P9-BAV-804

Croatia

Croatia

BY MARTIN HINTZ

Enchantment of the World
Second Series

WITHDRAWN

Children's Press®

A Division of Scholastic Inc.

NEW YORK TORONTO LONDON AUCKLAND SYDNEY
MEXICO CITY NEW DELHI HONG KONG
DANBURY, CONNECTICUT

Fitchburg Public Library
5530 Lacy Road
Fitchburg, WI 53711

Frontispiece: Bicycling in Croatia

Consultant: Ralph Bogert, Department of Slavic Languages and Literatures, University of Toronto, Ontario, Canada

Please note: *All statistics are as up-to-date as possible at the time of publication.*

Book production by Herman Adler Design

Library of Congress Cataloging-in-Publication Data

Hintz, Martin.
  Croatia / by Martin Hintz.
     p. cm. — (Enchantment of the world. Second series)
Includes bibliographical references and index.
     ISBN 0-516-24253-9
1. Croatia—Juvenile literature. [1. Croatia.] I. Title. II. Series.
  DR1510.H56 2004
  949.72—dc22   2003019635

© 2004 by Martin Hintz.
All rights reserved. Published in 2004 by Children's Press,
an imprint of Scholastic Library Publishing.
Published simultaneously in Canada.
Printed in China.

CHILDREN'S PRESS and associated logos are trademarks and or registered
trademarks of Scholastic Library Publishing. SCHOLASTIC and associated logos
are trademarks and or registered trademarks of Scholastic Inc.
4 5 6 7 8 9 10 R 13 12 11 10 09 08 07   62

Acknowledgments

For their insights on Croatia, the author would like to thank historians Francis D. Eterovich and Christoper Spalatin, librarian Marija Dalbello of Rutgers University, journalist Jeanne Oliver, filmmaker Frank M. Kicar, and writer Vladimir Blaskovic. Ivanka Luzmanovic, Natalie Mader, John Madigan, and Peter Schmidtke also deserve thanks for their help. And always, thanks to my wife, Pam, for her support and encouragement on this project. There's a nod, too, to my mother, Gertrude Hintz, who was a great companion during an exciting Croatian auto adventure that was grand fun, illuminating, and eye-opening.

To the displaced children and orphans of the Serbian-Croatian war of 1991.

Contents

Cover photo:
Roving Harbor,
Istria, Croatia

CHAPTER

Croatia's rolling hills

Zagreb Folk Festival

Hello to Croatia

8

SNOWCAPPED MOUNTAINS SNAGGING THE BRIGHT BLUE SKY. Clear waters of the Adriatic Sea washing the offshore islands. Historic ruins dotting the hillsides. Rushing traffic in large cities. Friendly kids waving from school yards. Croatia is a wonderful composite of modern and ancient, of harsh nature and warm people, of cool oak forests and golden hayfields, of soaring office buildings and crooked village lanes. It is a crossroads land fought over for centuries, with a wondrous history reaching deeply into ancient mists.

Opposite: **The Vinkovci Folklore Festival is a place where Croats can celebrate their heritage and culture.**

Gently rolling hills frame sprawling farmland in Croatia.

Long, long ago, the term *Croatian* was used to refer to two Slavic tribes living far beyond the borders of today's republic. The White Croats lived in Poland, along the upper reaches of the raging Visla River, with Krakow as their main fortress. Another tribe of Croats planted their crops and hunted in the northern and eastern parts of today's Czech Republic. Smaller groups of Croats mingled with other Slavic tribes such as the Slovenes and Slovaks, as well as with the Macedonians and perhaps even the Greeks in the far south. For years scholars debated intricate theories on the origin and meaning of the name Croat (*Hrvat*). One idea was suggested by the early Byzantine emperor Constantine VII Porphyrogenitus, an historian, who said the name came from the Greek word for land. A Croatian translation would be "people owning much land." Porphyrogenitus added that he believed the name was derived from the people living on the northern Adriatic island of Krk. In the nineteenth and twentieth centuries, other explanations were abundant. People variously claimed that Croat or Hrvat came from *hrev*, or "tree"; *hruv*, or "dance"; *heru*, or "sword"; or even *hruvat*, or "deer."

No Changes Planned

No matter where the term originated, the Croats are happy with who they are. They are fiercely proud of what their ancestors did to give them a wonderful heritage, one they love to share with others. Yet Croatia is no leftover land, a mere geographical backwater struggling to overcome a raucous history. As one of the world's newest nations, born in 1991 after centuries of strife, Croatia knows it has a future as bright as a July day at the seacoast.

Croats know there are plenty of challenges facing them as their nation strides into tomorrow. With the help of international business, cultural, and political communities, Croatia will certainly achieve its goals as a modern nation. Assistance also comes from Croatians around the world, whose downtrodden forebears emigrated years ago from their homeland to seek better lives elsewhere. Their dreams of a free and independent Croatia remained strong. And they never forgot their origins, wherever they moved. Young people still travel regularly from Croatia to the rest of the world, ready to share their talents and creativity. And more often, these days, they eagerly return home to Croatia brimming with ideas and concrete plans for building up their country. After all, they have a lot of heritage to emulate. Witness what some other Croats have done for their nation and for the world.

Juraj Dragisic (1445–1520) was a Franciscan priest born in the Bosnian town of Srebrenica. He advocated reform of the Julian calendar in 1514, and his work was accepted by Pope Gregory XIII in 1582. The Gregorian calendar has been in use in the West ever since. The ballpoint pen was invented in 1906 by Eduard Slavoljub Penkala (1871–1922).

A nation not even fifteen years old, Croatia's future is one of growth and pride.

Internationally known Antun Augustincic (1900–1979) produced the Monument of Peace sculpture that stands outside the United Nations building in New York City. Ivan Vucetic (1858–1925) was the first investigator to use fingerprint identification, a process called dactyloscopy. Vucetic was born on the Croatian island of Hvar and lived in Buenos Aires, Argentina, when he developed his technique. The police academy in La Plata now bears his name: Escuela de policia Juan Vucetic. Born in Zagreb, Fran Bosnjakovic (1902–1993) was one of the world's leading experts in thermodynamics.

Scientist Nikola Tesla (1856–1943) is credited with inventing numerous electronic devices and motors. He held more than 700 patents, many of which aided in the development of radio transmissions and improved lighting. Tesla came to the United States in 1884 with only a few cents in his pocket and some poems. Yet he went on to work closely with Thomas Edison, George Westinghouse, and other notable American business leaders who recognized his technological genius. Two other Croatian scientists are noted worldwide for their important discoveries in organic chemistry, for which they received Nobel Prizes. Lavoslav Ruzicka (1887–1976) was honored in 1939; Vladimir Prelog (1906–1998) received his award in 1975.

Yugoslavian-born Nikola Tesla

CROATIA

- ● Cities of over 50,000 people
- ○ Other cities
- ✪ National capital

0   50 miles

0   60 kilometers

AUSTRIA

Drava R.

Sava R.

SLOVENIA

HUNGARY

Varaždin

Koprivnica

Sesvete   Bjelovar

Zagreb   Virovitica

Drava R.

Kopacki Rit N.P.

Osijek

Danube R.

Karlovac   Sisak

Petrinja

Slavonska Požega

Dakovo

Vukovar

Risnjak N.P.

Opatija   Rijeka

Jasenovac

Slavonski Brod

Vinkovci

Krk

Brijuni N.P.

Plitvice Lakes N.P.

Pula

Cres

Paklenika N.P.

BOSNIA AND HERZEGOVINA

Nin

Zadar

Adriatic Sea

Otok

Krka R.   Knin

Krka N.P.

Kornati N.P.

Šibenik

ITALY

Trogir   Split

Brač

Makarska

Hvar

Croatia

Korčula

SERBIA AND MONTENEGRO

N

W   E

S

Dubrovnik

Geopolitical map of Croatia

Last, but not among the least, inventor Faust Vrancic (1551–1617) of Šibenik made the first parachute. He jumped off a building in Venice to test his device. It worked—just as Croatia works today.

Croatia's Rolling Geography

T HE LANDSCAPE OF CROATIA IS A LUMPY BLANKET, TOSSED with deep creases and high ridges. The country runs from the pillowed foothills of the Alps mountain range in the northwest to a wide plain in the east. Looking down at a map, Croatia's new-moon shape has often been compared with that of the pastry called a croissant. Compare the two after going to a bakery and then looking at a map.

Croatia lies in central Europe and has four neighbors. Its lengthy frontier runs 1,358 miles (2,185 kilometers). On the northwest is Slovenia with a ragged border running 416 miles (669 km). On the northeast is the 204-mile (328-km) border with Hungary. Serbia and Montenegro (formerly Yugoslavia) is to the east, with a frontier extending 158 miles (254 km). Bosnia and Herzegovina lie on the south, with its 579-mile (932-km) border. The smooth, blue waters of the warm Adriatic Sea lap along Croatia's rocky western shore.

There are three distinct geographical parts of Croatia: the coast, the mountains, and the Pannonian Plain. The total surface of Croatia covers 21,825 square miles (56,527 sq km). Of

Opposite: **Croatia's landscape is one of lofty mountains, rolling hills, plains, and coastal lowlands.**

The Adriatic meets the shores and harbors of Mljet Island off Croatia.

The highest peaks in Croatia are in the Dinaric Alps.

that, 21,781 square miles (56,413 sq km) is land, with an additional 11,991 square miles (31,057 sq km) of territorial waters. Croatia's claim extends 12 nautical miles (22 km) into the Adriatic. The nation is only slightly smaller than West Virginia and is drained by such major rivers as the Danube, Drava, Sava, Mura, Krapina, Kupa, Una, and Novcica.

In the center of the country, the Dinaric Alps trap the clouds and remain topped with snow for much of the year. They are the highest in Croatia at 6,004 feet (1,830 meters). The Velebit Range, part of the Dinaric Alps, comprises the longest stretch of mountains in Croatia and hugs the Adriatic coast. They arch from the cove of Senjska Draga and Vratnik to the upper Zrmanja River. The Velebit's total length is about 90 miles (145 km). These mountains consist of an extensive line of ridges and crests, separated by deep valleys. The tallest peaks of the northern Velebit lift their ragged, rocky heads up from the heart of Croatia. Mali Rajinac is the highest peak at

5,574 feet (1,699 m). Only a few mountain passes in this region have roads, narrow and twisting, that connect one valley with the next. The highway linking Karlovac and Senj is called Emperor Joseph's Road after a long-ago ruler of the Austro-Hungarian Empire in central Europe.

Mountains in the Heart of Croatia

The highest part of Velebit lies in the center of Croatia, east of the port city of Starigrad. The tallest mountain here is Vaganski Vrh at 5,751 feet (1,753 m). Under the stony face of another peak, Sveto Brdo (Holy Hill), the highway tunnel of Sveti Rok (Saint Roch) is under construction. Much of Croatia's landscape is karst, a porous limestone. Surface water leaks underground and forms fantastic caverns. Hundreds of caves pocket Velebit, the best known being Cerovacke Spilje (Cerovac Caves) near Gracac.

A mountain climber tackles the steep karst rockface of the Velebit range.

Velebit is also the most famous mountain range in Croatian history and culture. For centuries, visitors have been impressed with Velebit's scenic overlooks, hiking trails, and nature reserves. A national park there, Paklenica, is noted for its beauty. In 1978, Velebit Range was included by UNESCO in an international network of biosphere reserves.

Croatia's Geographic Features

Highest Elevation: Dinaric Alps, 6,004 feet (1,830 m)

Lowest Elevation: Adriatic Sea, sea level

Longest River: Sava River, 584 miles (940 km)

Largest Lake: Vrana, 74,379 acres (30,100 ha)

Largest City: Zagreb, 1,081,000 population

Highest Temperature: Summer along the Dalmatian coast, 79°F to 86°F (26°C to 30°C)

Lowest Temperature: Winter in the mountains, 23°F to 32°F (-5°C to 0°C)

Many National Parks

Croatia has an extensive system of national parks. One of the most popular is Risnjak, which was made a national park in 1953. Located in the western part of Gorski Kotar, the park is heavily forested with fir, spruce, and maple trees, making a cathedral-like setting. Its many shadowy woodland trails are accessible to young hikers interested in nature studies. This makes Risnjak a favorite locale for school outings. For a different landscape, Brijuni National Park consists of a clump of islands separated from the mainland by the Fazana Strait. The islands are covered with oak, laurel, pine, and olive trees. This

Croatia's Krka National Park is one of a vast network of national reserves.

Walkways allow visitors to the Plitvice lakes up-close views of waterfalls and azure water.

once was a resort for Yugoslavia's leaders under the old regime and is still a showcase for official visitors. An elephant even lived there once, part of a small zoo of exotic animals.

Photographers flock to the sixteen Plitvice lakes (Plitvicka Jezera). The upper lakes are particularly photogenic, surrounded by heavy woods with waterfalls tumbling down the steep slopes. Although the region was not made into a national park until 1949, the first lodge here was built in 1862, and the first hotel opened in 1896.

Mapping the Sea Coast

Mapping seaside Croatia must have been a maddening experience. Imagine the big job of counting and measuring all the country's bays, inlets, and outcroppings. The official figure for the entire length of coastline is 3,617 miles (5,820 km), including 2,515 miles (4,046 km) of island and reef coastline. There are 1,185 islands off coastal Croatia, with the largest island being Krk at 178 square miles (461 sq km). Only sixty-seven of these rocky pinpricks are inhabited, mostly by fishermen and their families.

The Kornati Islands comprise the largest and most dense archipelago in the Adriatic Sea. An archipelago is a large cluster of islands. This chain of rocks consists of 147 islands scattered over 90 square miles (233 sq km) of the sea. One of

The Kornati Islands rise out of the Adriatic Sea

Croatia's Environmental Concerns

Croatia has many natural resources, in addition to a well-developed system of protected districts. Its soil is fertile, and the country is fortunate to have relatively uncontaminated waters. Yet there are still environmental challenges affecting this small country, similar to those throughout Europe. The primary issues include air pollution from metallurgical plants. Damage to forests from acid rain is also of concern to environmentalists. There is growing coastal pollution as a result of industrial and domestic waste. The State Directorate for Nature and Environmental Protection is responsible for regulating and protecting Croatia's natural resources.

the richest fishing grounds in the Adriatic lies offshore. Humans settled here as early as the Stone Age. Today, boaters love spending nights bobbing at anchor offshore and enjoying the moon under the clear, dark sky. Visitors can then spend the next day exploring the islands' caves. Some vacationers rent stone cottages on the islands for their getaways.

With its mountains, seaside, and inland hills, Croatia has several temperature zones. Northern Croatia has a cool, fresh continental climate. Central Croatia has a semihighland and highland climate. The Croatian coast has balmy, sunny Mediterranean weather. Winter temperatures range from 30° Fahrenheit to 86°F (-1° Celsius to 30°C) in the continental region, 23°F to 32°F (-5°C to 0°C) in the mountain region, and 41°F to 50°F (5°C to 10°C) in the coastal region. Summer temperatures range from 72°F to 79°F (22°C to 26°C) in the continental region, 59°F to 68°F (15°C to 20°C) in the mountain region, and 79°F to 86°F (26°C to 30°C) in the coastal region. Croatia averages 2,600 hours of sunlight each year, making it one of the sunniest countries of Europe. On the other hand, the winter's snow is a great attraction for

Palm trees become covered in snow as a winter storm passes through Split.

skiers, with slopes piled with up to 44 inches (112 centimeters) of the fluffy white stuff. Annual rainfall is 26 inches (66 cm).

Croatia's winds have always had a great impact on the country's weather and have affected its lifestyle as a seafaring nation. In the days of sail, mariners on the Adriatic needed to be aware of all these winds and how they blew so that they could safely maneuver their lumbering merchant ships or sleek military vessels. The wind is usually light to moderate between September and June. However, storms can often rise quickly in July and August. Even today, recreational sailors in their expensive yachts need to be aware of these weather changes.

Since the Croats remain akin to the sea and the elements that affect its many moods, they have named the winds. The refreshing *mistral* of the spring and summer can create brush-fire problems along the seacoast as it slowly dries out the underbrush and trees. This daytime wind blows in from the sea and crosses the land. It is caused by temperature differences between the water and ground. When these temperatures vary greatly, the mistral blows harder. However, it is generally mild as it swirls around the Mediterranean basin and up the Adriatic Sea.

The *bora*, sometimes called the bura, regularly occurs in the summer. This strong northeast wind blows across the mainland and out to sea from sunset to sunrise and is also caused by varying temperatures between the land and water. The bora is usually not as strong as the mistral. An easterly bora, called a *levanter*, brings rain and cold to the northern Adriatic. The *tramontane* is a milder bora but very unpredictable, blowing from the north to affect the southern Adriatic.

The *sirocco* is a humid, warm breeze blowing up from North Africa. It is the primary wind along the Croatian coast from May through September. It causes choppy seas, rainy weather, and thick clouds.

Other winds are more dangerous. The gale-force *lebic* roars in from the southwest, bringing heavy rain and causing huge waves that sometimes cause serious damage when they smash against the Croatian coast. The *nevera* is a heavy squall, a short storm that blows in from the west. These violent summer storms can arise quickly, accompanied by rolls of thunder and stark flashes of lightning. They blow over quickly, leaving comfortable, cooler air in their wake. These storms, common from June through September, drift across the Adriatic from Italy to hit only a small area of water before dissipating. Such gales are rare in the winter. With experience and training, a good sailor can deal with all these weather changes.

Looking at Croatia's Cities

Split is the second most important city in Croatia, with about 172,700 residents who are called Splicani. Split was originally a Greek outpost, dating at least 400 years before Christ. The Roman emperor Diocletian built an enormous palace there in A.D. 295 (below). While some parts of the building's original architecture have been altered, most of the structure remains as it was when he lived here. The city, called Spalatum before it became known as Split, is full of ancient churches, houses, gates, walls, and other architectural works. Among its notable museums are the Maritime Museum and the Museum of Croatian Archaeological

Monuments. Over the centuries the city was controlled by Venetians, Austrians, French, and Italians. It has pleasant coastal weather.

The walled merchant city of Dubrovnik (above) (earlier called Ragusa) was an independent republic for 700 years. The streets, forts, and ramparts look as they did in the Middle Ages. Much of the architecture from the Middle Ages was destroyed, however, in a terrible 1667 earthquake, and was replaced by buildings with more ornate designs. Visitors enter through the Pile Gate and walk along the Stradun, the main street, to look in the shop windows. Among the city's notable buildings are the Prince's Palace, the church of Saint Vlaho, the city hall, and several monasteries. A central square called the Gunduliceva Poljana hosts a busy outdoor market each morning in the growing season. One of the oldest continuously operating pharmacies is found in Dubrovnik. During a war with Yugoslavia in 1991 and 1992, parts of the ancient city were damaged. The international community helped with its repairs. Dubrovnik is the most southeasterly city in Croatia and enjoys pleasant temperatures.

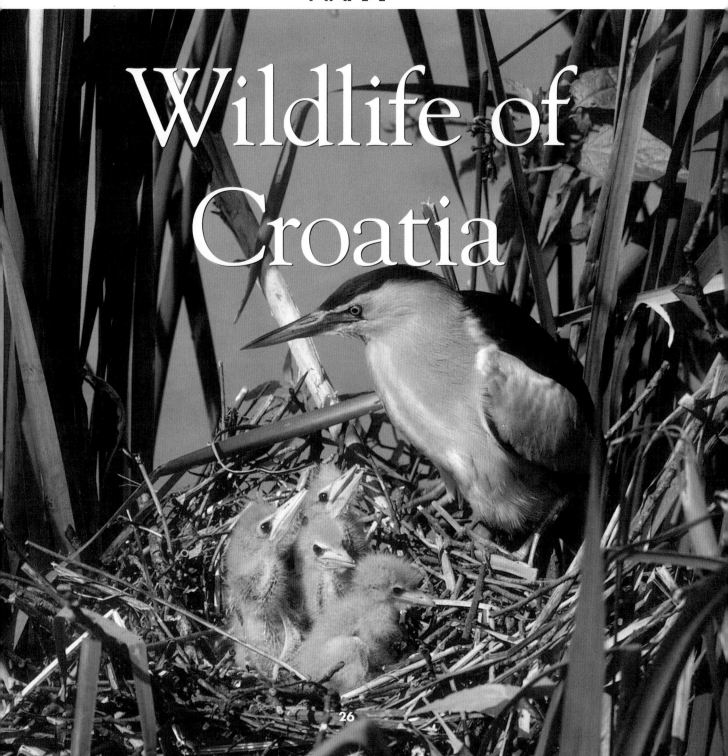

Wildlife of Croatia

CROATIA HAS A NOAH'S ARK OF ANIMALS LIVING IN ITS mountains, along the many waterways, on the plains, and in the forests. The extensive range of vegetation throughout the country provides a safe haven for a large variety of creeping, crawling, walking, running, and flying creatures. Croatia's lakes and rivers, as well as the offshore waters of the Adriatic Sea, teem with fish of many sorts.

Opposite: **Bird life is abundant in Croatia.**

A Birdwatcher's Paradise

Croatia is situated at the crossroads of Europe, the Far East, and Africa. Ancient merchants traveled back and forth between these worlds, using well-established routes through the mountains and along the sea. In the same way, migrating birds also find their way to Croatia.

Kopacki Rit is a nature park not far from where the Drava and the Danube rivers merge. Near the city of Osijek in eastern Croatia, the park is one of the most important intact wetlands in Europe. Its many backwaters and pools attract hungry waterfowl. Eager scientists roam the region to study the zoological reserve and its 260 species of nesting birds. Among them are wild geese, bitterns, and varieties of ducks. In addition, there are graceful white herons, long-legged storks, jabbering crows, warblers, coots, gull, terns, and several types of rat-tat-tatting woodpeckers. Kopacki Rit is also an important nesting site for gangly spoonbills and long-legged

Croatia's marshlands are home to the black kite.

The wetlands of Croatia's nature parks attract many birds, including the egret.

cranes, which poke around the weedy shallows seeking minnows. Migrating birds flock here in the spring and autumn. Also at home here are fierce raptors like black kites and rare white-tailed eagles that find excellent feeding opportunities in the marshlands.

The meadows and pastures of Lonjsko Polje, another nature park, are the habitat of eagles, white egrets, grey herons, and endangered black storks. There are about 600 nesting pairs of storks living in the park, home to the greatest concentration of these birds in

Europe. To reproduce, they need mature, undisturbed forest with plenty of streams, ponds, and wetlands. Perfect for these birds, Lonjsko Polje is part of a wide, muddy floodplain spreading between the Sava River and Moslavacka Gora Mountain along the Lonja River.

Life Under Croatia's Waters

With its variety of waterways, Croatia has an abundance of fish species. On inland lakes and rivers, anglers try their luck going for pike, bream, carp, catfish, perch, eels, and mullet. The lowlands in the Lonjsko Polje are often flooded for six months of the year, providing a safe hatching ground for giant pike. The scrappy bluefin tuna is one of the most sought-after big game fish in the Adriatic. It is a huge species that can weigh more than 1,400 pounds (630 kilograms). There is a growing number of broadbill swordfish. They leap out of the

The waterways off of Croatia's coast host large fish, such as tuna.

Croatian fishermen sort the day's catch.

water and fall back with a great splash. Sometimes blue sharks and thresher sharks are caught. Albacore, mahi-mahi, and amberjack can be found on the western sides of many of Croatia's islands. Smaller fish like anchovies and sardines are plentiful, as are lobsters and squid. For centuries, hardy Croatian fishermen have fished these clear waters for their livelihood. European sportfishing championships are regularly held off the rugged coastline, with competitors eager to try their luck. They use the fanciest rods and reels, tantalizing lures, depth gauges, and other devices.

Far below the waves, scuba divers find rainbowed schools of brilliantly colored fish swimming through the reefs and scooting in and out of the many shipwrecks. The *Baron Gautsch* is one such sunken vessel. It went down in 1914 during World War I when it hit an underwater mine, killing 177 persons on board. Today, it is a favorite site to explore, but only with a permit and under the watchful eye of a guide who knows all the potential dangers on such an expedition.

A scuba diver examines the wreck of a World War II torpedo boat of the coast of Croatia.

The sheer walls of underwater canyons are decorated with crimson and yellow coral, making them perfect subjects for photographers with special cameras. Deep-water diving has a long tradition in Croatia. Since the late 1800s, sponge divers from Krapanj Island have braved the deep Adriatic waters. They wore heavy helmets, filled with air pumped down long hoses from the surface. The first diving clubs, started in the 1950s, attracted members from around the world. Now there are at least 130 such organizations and 150 diving centers in the country. Excursion boats take vacationers far offshore because the rocky coastline makes it dangerous to dive close to land.

Dolphins in Danger

Hrvoje Gomercic, a professor on the veterinary faculty of Zagreb University, has been collecting information on the Adriatic's dolphins. Due to his efforts, the dolphins have been a protected species since 1995. Dolphins are constantly threatened by fishing nets, high-speed boats, Jet Skis, and disease. A deadly fungus affecting the dolphins is especially worrisome to scientists.

Scientists are also monitoring the spread of *Caulerpa taxifolia*, a fast-growing, bothersome type of algae, which has disturbed the natural balance of fish and vegetation in the Adriatic.

A forest-roaming animal, pine martens find their home in Croatia's wooded hills.

Forest and Farm Animals

On land, many mammal species call Croatia their home. Deer and wild boar roam the wooded hills, while wildcats and pine martens search for food in the underbrush. Exotic fur-bearing animals include the weasel and the sable. Krka National Park is one of the last Mediterranean habitats of water-loving otters. The deep, dark caves here are inhabited by eighteen species of bats. Croatia has insects, too, such as dragonflies and damselflies. Snapping at the buzzing bugs are lizards sunning on the rocks, while frogs splash in the wetlands. Turtles float on the backwaters, crawling slowly up onto partially submerged logs when they need to rest. Two dangerous snake species in Croatia are the poisonous horned viper and the European adder. The leopard and grass snakes are nonpoisonous.

A poisonous snake in Croatia is the horned viper.

Sheepdogs and Dalmations

One species of energetic shaggy sheepdog is native to Croatia. In addition to its herding tasks, it makes an excellent watchdog. First mention of these animals was in 1374, when Petar, bishop of Djakovo, described the curly, black-haired dog distinguished by its foxlike face. Proud owners say that their little dogs can even identify individual sheep and cattle if they have been given names!

These well-trained sheepdogs can follow either hand or voice commands as they go about their work on the wide plains of Slavonia, an historic region northeast of Zagreb. Even a nod of the herder's head can be a signal. They are brave enough to face down snorting bulls, ignoring the horns and pawing hooves, when it is time for the cattle to be penned. Sometimes, the dogs are used to drive pigs into Croatia's oak groves for their autumn feeding. When the farmer determines it is time to retrieve his fattened porkers, the dogs then race back into the woods to find the hogs hiding in the deep underbrush.

The Croatians like to say that they are the nation of one-hundred-and-one Dalmatians. First, they refer to the dozens of islands off the coast of Dalmatia. Second,

they are talking about the famous white dogs with black-spotted coats (above). For several years, the Croatian embassy in Washington, D.C., even had one of the friendly animals as its live-in mascot. The origin of this breed is debated. Pictures of similar dogs were found in Egyptian tombs and on Greek monuments, so they have been in existence for many centuries. Dalmatians became the work dogs of Europe by the nineteenth century and were usually used as watchdogs, often running alongside carriages to protect the passengers from bandits. Their skill in hunting rats kept the stables free of vermin. Today, high-spirited Dalmatians are mascots at fire departments, perform in circuses, and are great family pets.

Farms in Croatia have the typical array of animals: cows, pigs, chickens, sheep, and other domesticated creatures. Although rare, the spotted Turopolje swine is among the hog species. This pig, with its multicolored black and yellow skin, is easy to handle and can make its home even in marshy areas. The animal is an excellent meat producer, first raised in the

A Protected Horse Breed

The beautiful Posavac horse is a protected breed found only in Croatia. The city of Klostar, about a twenty-minute drive from Zagreb, is the seat of the Federation of Croatian Posavac Horse Breeeders Associations.

The group works to preserve and improve the dark, high-stepping horses traditionally used to pull carriages and farm wagons. The Posavac is also protected in Croatia's Lonjsko Polje Nature Park.

mid-1300s. Improved breeding techniques that began in the 1800s strengthened the species. The Slavonian black hog is nearly extinct, but some are still found in Croatia.

Most of Croatia's farms have dairy cattle rather than beef cattle. Although there are about 19,000 family farms, they average one to three cows each, with only sixteen farms having more than 130 head. There are some 438,000 head of cattle throughout the country today. The main breeds are the milk-heavy Simmental and Holstein-Friesian.

Edelweiss is a rare find in the Velebit Mountains.

Mountain Pines to Marsh Grass

Croatia's vegetation ranges from reeds in marshy meadows to pine trees on the lower slopes of the mountains. The Velebit Mountains have a rich array of plants that delight botanists who have counted more than 2,700 species growing there. Among the rare flowers is the beautiful, fragile edelweiss. Other species include orchids, lilies, and a plant that is actually very pretty despite its name of hairy alpenrose. The spreading branches of chestnut, hornbeam, ash, willow, oak, and poplar trees are seen throughout the country. Cliffsides are home to some forty herbal species, the most important of which is the Dubrovnik cornflower. The tree spurge is another interesting

A lavender field sweeps Croatian hills.

herblike plant, the only such species in Croatia. There are at least thirty-six varieties of moss.

Because there is such diversity in Croatia's landscapes, plants have adapted well. For instance, Mount Ucka, the highest peak on the Istrian Peninsula, is an important climatic barrier. When the wind hits the slopes, air masses are forced to rise. This causes considerable rainfall for the low-lying forests. With its rich vegetation, Ucka is very different from other peaks in the Primorje region. Croatia's coastal belt is blanketed with typical Mediterranean vegetation. Laurel is the most abundant. Also found here are fragrant oleander, jasmine, and lavender.

Protecting Plants and Animals

Interest in the environment is nothing new in Croatia. First attempts at environmental protection began in the early 1900s. They led to the establishment of Croatia's first national parks, Velebit and Plitvice Lakes, in 1928. *Nature* magazine

The Croatian Ecological Society ensures the protection of the nation's wildlife. One threat is overforestation.

was launched in 1911 by the Croatian Society of Natural Sciences. The Croatian Ecological Society, begun in 1969, makes sure that the country is aware of challenges in protecting its natural resources. Increased support for environmental causes was part of a worldwide trend of the early 1980s, when many Croats became worried over threats to the country's wildlife, vegetation, waterways, and air. School groups, college students, and ordinary citizens researched problems and helped to come up with money and helping hands to keep their country green and free of pollution. They also worked closely with activists in other countries by sharing ideas and strategies. Scientists and other experts contributed their insights and skills, consulting with governmental agencies and businesses. The Croatian Green Alliance often coordinates the activities of many environmental groups.

Groups such as the Croatian Ecological Society, Green Action, the Young Nature Keepers of the Croatian Society of Natural Science, and The Only Planet continue to actively protect the environment. Youngsters help by planting trees and building birdhouses. They also make field trips to protected sites such as the Biokovo Botanical Garden, established in 1984 to promote the conservation of the mountainous area's plant life.

The garden, founded with the help of noted herb specialist and collector Jure Radic, is located in the village of Kotisina. Another well-known botanical facility is found along the highway between the cities of Split and Trogir. Students and their teachers at the Vjeko Butir school began planting these gardens in 1976, emphasizing Mediterranean-type flowers and medicinal plants. The children also installed thirteen varieties of sprawling olive trees in their tidy 5.6-acre (2.3-hectare) plot adjacent to the school building. In addition to native species, other trees were donated from France, Italy, and Spain. In 1986, the government protected the school garden by calling it an horticultural monument.

One of the oldest gardens in Croatia is the 63-acre (25.5-ha) Trsteno Arboretum near Dubrovnik. The site was established at the end of the fifteenth century as a park and summer residence of a wealthy family. In 1948, the complex was donated to the Croatian Academy of Sciences and Arts. More than 300 species of plants are still found there, although the main arboretum building was heavily damaged in the 1991 war with Yugoslavia.

Plant life on the mountainous slopes of Croatia is protected by several ecological societies.

History and Heritage

Humans have lived in what is now Croatia since the dim, early days of the Stone Age. In a cave near Krapina in northwestern Croatia, archaeologists have found evidence of humans dating back at least 100,000 years. Since the area lay along the sea routes and was on accessible land pathways, many cultures made their trails back and forth across this landscape.

The written history of Croatia started when the Greeks established colonies along the Dalmatian coast as early as 580 B.C. The interior was populated by tribal peoples, with the Celts being most powerful. The Celtic Norican Kingdom, which incorporated today's Austria, Slovenia, and portions of northern Croatia, eventually fell to the Romans after 300 B.C. It then became the province of Pannonia. Remains of Roman roads and watchtowers can still be seen in today's Croatia. Slavic tribes from Poland then made their way south to Croatia in the early A.D. 600s. The Croatians adopted Christianity around 800.

Opposite: **Neanderthal bones, discovered in a Krapina cave, are now housed in Zagreb's Museum of Natural History.**

Remains from Croatia's days under Roman rule still stand. This is a Roman amphitheater.

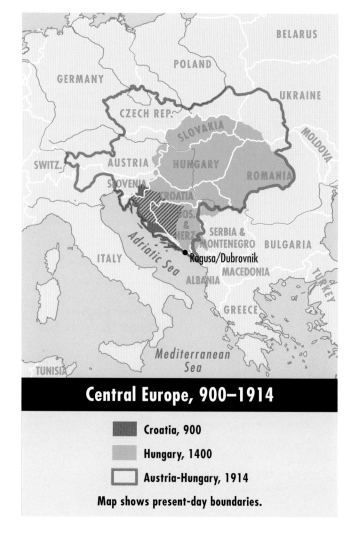

Central Europe, 900–1914

- ■ Croatia, 900
- ▨ Hungary, 1400
- ☐ Austria-Hungary, 1914

Map shows present-day boundaries.

Princely Power

At this time, various strongmen controlled the lands around their fortified houses. They set up their own estates along the Adriatic coast and inland in Slavonia. Between 910 and 914, Prince Tomislav solidified his rule over Croatia's Dalmatian coastline and united with Slavonia (once Roman Pannonia). He was crowned Croatia's first king in 925. When Tomislav died, civil wars weakened what remained of the old central authority, and all of Croatia's outlying territories were lost.

In the late 900s and into the next century, control of the coastline swung between the Byzantine Empire and Venice, a powerful merchant city on the nearby Italian peninsula. However, Ragusa (today's Dubrovnik) was a rival trading power. Ragusa maintained close ties to the Byzantines to escape being taken over by the powerful Venetian navy. By 1090, Venetian power was strong enough along most of the coast to occupy and rule all of the major cities and islands for several centuries. Yet Venice was still not able to take over Ragusa/Dubrovnik, which had developed into an independent city-state with its own merchant ships trading all over Europe, including London, England, in the far north.

A Scramble for Power

King Zvonimir died in 1089 without any sons to replace him. The last elected Croatian king, Peter Svacic, ruled from 1093 to 1097. After his death, a group of Croatian nobles signed the Pacta Conventa in 1102 with King Koloman of Hungary. They allowed him to wear the Croatian crown so that he would leave them alone. Other Croatians, however, violently opposed this union with Hungary.

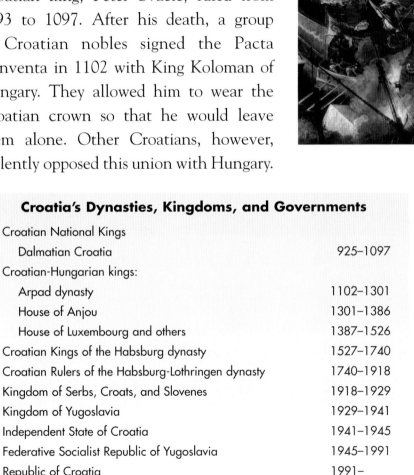

The Venetian navy was a strong force as it overtook ports along the Adriatic coast.

Croatia's Dynasties, Kingdoms, and Governments

Croatian National Kings	
Dalmatian Croatia	925–1097
Croatian-Hungarian kings:	
Arpad dynasty	1102–1301
House of Anjou	1301–1386
House of Luxembourg and others	1387–1526
Croatian Kings of the Habsburg dynasty	1527–1740
Croatian Rulers of the Habsburg-Lothringen dynasty	1740–1918
Kingdom of Serbs, Croats, and Slovenes	1918–1929
Kingdom of Yugoslavia	1929–1941
Independent State of Croatia	1941–1945
Federative Socialist Republic of Yugoslavia	1945–1991
Republic of Croatia	1991–

They were defeated by the Hungarians, and Koloman was crowned King of Croatia, Slavonia, and Dalmatia in 1102.

For the next several hundred years, Croatia was ruled by a succession of Croatian-Hungarian kings, most of whom were of the Arpad dynasty. To solidify their power, the kings gave land to nobles in exchange for their allegiance. Such strong families as the Frankapan and Subic clans grew very powerful as their territories expanded over the years. In southern Croatia, these wealthy families eventually became very independent and began grabbing property from their weaker neighbors. At first, the kings ignored what was happening, but eventually they retaliated by lowering the value of currency and instigated other rules that the upper classes disliked. As a result, the nobles rebelled in 1222 and forced King Andrija II (Andrew II) to issue the "Golden Bull," a charter that placed limits on the crown's authority. Among its points, the document demanded that the king call an assembly, the Sabor, every year to hear complaints. The nobles reserved the right to object if he didn't respond to their requests.

Bas-relief of a Croatian king

In the twelfth and thirteenth centuries, the kings invited Italian and German craft workers and merchants to live in Croatia. Protected by the king, these "guests" were encouraged to help build towns along important trade routes and near castles in the interior of the country where they could then practice their trades. To promote development, several communities earned royal charters granting freedom to expand without interference from the court or local nobles. Gradec, which today is part of Zagreb, was one such town. Among their privileges, artisans and traders from these communities did not have to pay customs duties when they traveled between markets. They also were given permission to organize fairs, boisterous gatherings that attracted musicians, jugglers, ropewalkers, and other entertainers, as well as traders and merchants. In exchange for these opportunities, the towns were responsible for their own defense. They had to pay for the construction of strong, high walls around their homes and shops, as well as to fund security forces.

With the emphasis on trade throughout the Adriatic, the coastal cities also grew stronger. Dubrovnik had become one of Europe's most powerful merchant communities by the thirteenth century. Shipbuilding, making leather and wine, and olive oil processing were among its major industries. As the city enlarged and grew more independent, streets were paved, a sewer system was installed, and orphanages and hospitals were established. Dubrovnik also

As trade increased, Dubrovnik grew into a powerful merchant community.

set up the first quarantine system in Europe, whereby travelers to the city had to wait a specified time before being allowed through the gates. This helped prevent the spread of disease.

In 1301, the Arpad dynasty finally died out, to be replaced by the kings of Naples, who were part of the House of Anjou from France. The first Anjou king was Charles Robert, who reigned until 1342. Yet by the middle of the 1300s, trouble was already looming. In an ongoing civil war, the nobles constantly fought with each other and the king. Cities were carelessly built and were very dirty, ravaged by plagues and devastating fires. Adding to the problems, neighboring Venice began taking over Croatian territories in the northwest and southeast.

The invasion of Sultan Suleyman and his army at the Battle of Mohács

From the east, the entire Adriatic was threatened by the growing power of the Ottoman Empire as it spread outward from Turkey in the 1400s. Under this pressure, many Croats fled to places where they thought they would be safer, such as Austria, Hungary, and Slovakia. Today, all that remains of these refugees are the family names still prevalent in some of those far-flung communities.

In 1522, the Croatian nobility asked Archduke Ferdinand of Habsburg, Austria, for help in blocking the invasion of a mighty Turkish army. In 1526, the Muslim Turks defeated the Christian Hungarians at Mohács, a bloody battle in which King Louis II of Hungary was killed. In his place, Ferdinand of Habsburg was elected king of Hungary and Croatia in 1527. In 1553 one of Ferdinand's Austrian generals was placed in charge of the border regions of Croatia and Slavonia. He hired refugees to fill out his garrisons. This led to the establishment of a stretch of Serb-settled territory between the Habsburgs and the Turkish lands. Under separate military commands, these Serbian districts grew stronger over the years. The settlements were far from the Croatian authorities in Zagreb and remained more or less independent until late in the nineteenth century. Venice held on to Dalmatia until 1797, when Emperor Napoleon of France conquered the Venetian Republic. In 1808, the Republic of Ragusa (Dubrovnik) was also absorbed by France.

Seeking Independence

The Illyrian Movement, which sought total independence for Croatia and other Slavic communities, including Serbia, was formed by the Croatian poet Ljudevit Gaj in 1835. But it was the Hungarian revolution (1848–1849) against the Habsburgs that allowed the Croatian *ban* (governor), Baron Josip Jelacic, to assert Croatia's separate status.

Croatian leader Ante Starcevic left the Illyrian Movement after 1848 and founded the Party of Rights to

Baron Josip Jelacic

Kingdom of the Serbs, Croats, and Slovenes, 1919

Above right: **King Alexander I joined the Serbs and the Slovenes, renaming the country Yugoslavia.**

advocate an independent Croatia that included Bosnia in the south. Starcevic was an extreme Croatian nationalist who fought for full independence from Austria and Hungary and wanted to unite other Slavic peoples under a Croation state.

After World War I, when the Habsburg Empire collapsed in 1918, the Croatian National Council took over in Zagreb. The council sought a union with other Slavs in the old empire and supported the establishment of the Kingdom of the Serbs, Croats, and Slovenes. The kingdom was to be headquartered in Belgrade, the seat of Serbian power. The Serbs eagerly legitimized their power in the Vidovdan Constitution of 1921. Of course, this was not received well by the other nationalities in the fledgling kingdom. In Croatia, resistance was led by the

Croatian Peasants Party under Stjepan Radić, a popular politician. In 1928, Radić was assassinated in Belgrade's Parliament building. In 1929, King Alexander of Yugoslavia united a separate Croatia with its neighbors, the Serbs and the Slovenes. He renamed the country Yugoslavia. Naturally, there was continued Croatian resistance to this centralization. But a compromise was reached in 1939 with the establishment of an individual Croatian *banovina* (province).

Rolling War Clouds

War clouds were again rolling across Europe by now, with the rise of the German Nazi (National Socialist) fascist party. In 1941, Yugoslavia was invaded by a huge force of Germans, Italians, and Hungarians. The Nazis allowed a fascist Croatian organization, the Ustashe, to assemble an Independent State of

Independent Croatia, 1941

- Axis Power
- Axis Power ally
- Under Axis occupation
- → Axis offensive

During World War II, the Croatian militia organized the Ustashe and the Independent State of Croatia.

Croatia. This new "country" included Croatia and all of Bosnia under the administration of a dictator named Ante Pavelić. Some Croatian soldiers joined the German war effort and fought primarily in Russia. Thousands of other Croatians who objected to the Nazis were imprisoned and murdered.

Rebels who favored a Russian style of communism were led by Josip Broz Tito. A Croat, Tito was born in Kumrovec, a town near Zagreb. He became a radical union organizer in the Croatian capital in the 1920s and 1930s. Tito was a careful military strategist who used his connections with the Soviet Union and the British to edge out rival rebel groups fighting the Nazis. When the Nazis were finally defeated in 1945, the Communists set up a new Yugoslavia, a federal state of six republics, consisting of Croatia, Serbia, Slovenia, Bosnia and Herzegovina, Macedonia, and Montenegro. The autonomous regions of Kosovo and Vojvodina were controlled by Serbia. Tito was to act as the federal president, with the Yugoslav capital at Belgrade. He became a leader of a movement of non-aligned nations during the cold war, the era after World War II when the United States and its friends opposed the Soviet Union and its allies. Some nations, such as Yugoslavia, preferred to remain more or less neutral in this face-off.

Josip Broz Tito, leader of Yugoslav patriots

Cardinal Speaks Out for Freedom

Cardinal Alojzije Stepinac (1898–1960) was the archbishop of Zagreb and an important Croatian historian who publicly condemned the Nazis and their Ustashe supporters during World War II. Despite his outspoken courage on behalf of the Croatian people, he was imprisoned by the Communists. He died in prison, and the Roman Catholic Church proclaimed him a martyr for his faith. Pope John Paul II beatified Stepinac on October 3, 1998. This is one of the steps the church takes before canonization, which means declaring someone a saint.

There were many political disturbances throughout the late 1960s. Street demonstrations and actual battles with police resulted in the arrests of numerous Croatian leaders. This rigid system broke down after Tito died in 1980. He had tried to prevent the taking control of the country by any one republic by setting up a rotating presidency that would operate after his death.

Each of the six republics, plus Kosovo and Vojvodina, was supposed to have its representative elected as federal president for a year. This worked briefly, but it also weakened

Yugoslavia, 1945–1989

Above left: **Slobodan Milošević**

Above right: **The elections in 1990 were won by the Croatian Democratic Union. Franjo Tudjman was elected president.**

the power of the president. This situation did not become obvious until the Serbs, and especially Slobodan Milošević, a Serb and the president of Yugoslavia, began to openly trumpet extreme nationalist policies in 1987 and 1988. None of the other ethnic groups in the federation felt strong enough to contain the Serbs.

Candidates for the 1990 elections in Croatia included both Croatian nationalists and non-nationalists. But the nearby Serbian media was under Milošević's watchful eye. His newspapers and radio broadcasts claimed that the Croatian candidates advocated a return to the terrible days when the Ustashe were in power. The radical media inflamed Serbs in Croatia to be ready to defend themselves. Nevertheless, the Croatian Democratic Union party, led by strongman Franjo Tudjman, won, and a new constitution was drawn up that December.

The Yugoslav federal government began unraveling. Serbs still advocated central federal control and were supported in this by the army. The military worried that the breakdown of Communist Party control would cut back their privileged position in Yugoslav society. Yet Croatian politicians, along with the Slovenes, suggested that the governmental system be changed to that of a loose federation or even a confederation, which is more of an alliance of independent countries. Bosnia and Macedonia generally took a middle position on the issue. Montenegro backed the Serbs, as did Kosovo and Vojvodina. This meant that the Serbs now had four out of the eight votes in the federal government. Because of this and related political issues, both Slovenia and Croatia declared their independence on June 25, 1991.

Unlike Slovenia, Croatia had a large Serbian minority. President Milošević did not really care what Slovenia did, but he warned that the Serb areas of Croatia would break away if Croatia deserted Yugoslavia. Since the Serbs controlled the Yugoslav army, the Croatians were at a disadvantage when fighting eventually broke out. As a result, Serbs captured about one-third of Croatia between June 1991 and early January 1992, when a cease-fire was set up. They

War-damaged homes and roads were a result of the 1991–92 fighting.

proclaimed the Republic of Serbian Krajina, which included the land routes to the coastal cities and tourist sites, most of Croatia's oil resources, and the cutting of the major highway between Zagreb and Slavonia. Serb shelling severely damaged the old city of Dubrovnik, to the world's great distress.

Help from the United Nations

The United Nations intervened in 1992 and stopped most of the fighting. Yet the Croats objected to the resulting stalemate. By 1994, the Croatian government wanted the United

Aiding in the cease-fire, United Nations armored vehicles line a Croatian street.

CONFÉRENCE DE PAIX SUR L'EX-YOUGOSLAVIE
PARIS

Nations to leave, despite opposition from the rest of Europe. Croatia took matters into its own hands in 1995, and its own military recaptured much of its territory once held by the Serbs. In the autumn, the Croatian army helped the Bosnians push Bosnian Serb forces out of western Bosnia-Herzegovina. Another cease-fire, established in October, opened the door to the Bosnian peace accord signed on December 14, 1995.

On December 14, 1995, Balkan leaders (seated) gathered in Paris, France, to sign a treaty ending one of Europe's most devastating wars.

History and Heritage **53**

Democratic Rule at Last

C ROATIA IS PROUD TO CALL ITSELF A PARLIAMENTARY democracy after long, painful years of occupations, dictatorships, and single-party rule. The government is organized on the principle of the separation of powers into legislative, executive, and judicial branches, as in the United States and Canada.

Opposite: **The Croatian flag hangs from a government building in Zagreb.**

Croatian National Flag

Over the centuries, Croatia has had numerous flags, depending upon the ruling power at the time. The assorted provinces, districts, and cities each had their own flags, too. Just as the boundaries of what constituted Croatia ebbed and flowed, the flag also changed designs. Many of these variations are exhibited in the Croatian Historical Museum in Zagreb. As a revolutionary symbol, the current tricolor flag dates back to about 1848.

The flag's red, white, and blue colors are based on the ancient banners of Red Croatia, White Croatia, and the Kingdom of Slavonia. Red and White Croatia were states in the early Middle Ages, approximately located in today's Dalmatia and central Croatia (red), and in Bosnia and Herzegovina (white). Slavonia is represented by the blue. According to the writer Miroslav Krleza, the colors represent the blood of Croatian martyrs, Croatia's peaceful lamblike nature, and Croatian devotion to God.

The basic flag was adopted after World War I by the newly formed Kingdom of Serbs, Croats, and Slovenes (1918–1929). In 1938 the tricolor was altered somewhat by placing the country's white and red coat-of-arms shield in the center. When the nation was the People's Republic of Croatia (1945–1963) and then a socialist republic (1963–1990), a red star symbolizing revolution was prominently displayed in the middle of the flag. The coat of arms is currently back again in the center of the flag, and the red star has been retired.

The executive branch consists of a chief of state, called the president, and a prime minister, who is the head of government. The prime minister is assisted by three deputy prime ministers: a first deputy, a second one responsible for the economy, and a third for social affairs. The cabinet, called the Council of Ministers, is chosen by the prime minister and must be approved by the Parliament (the Sabor).

Stjepan Mesic, President of Croatia

Stjepan Mesic was born on December 24, 1934, in Orahovica. He was involved in politics as a young man, especially as a student leader at the University of Zagreb. After receiving his law degree, Mesic became a member of Parliament in the Socialist Republic of Croatia. In the early 1970s, he served a one-year prison term for advocating Croatia's equality within the Yugoslavia federation.

In the early 1990s Mesic joined the Croatian Democratic Union and eventually became chairman of its executive committee. He was appointed the country's first prime minister and served as Croatia's member in the Presidency of the Socialist Federal Republic of Yugoslavia until 1991.

From 1992 to 1994 Mesic served as speaker of the Parliament of the independent Republic of Croatia. He became active in several other political parties and was elected president of Croatia in 2000 with 56 percent of the vote. Mesic speaks fluent Russian and French. He is married and has two daughters.

Each Sunday Mesic invites Croatian citizens to visit him in the presidential villa on a hill overlooking Zagreb. The president is well known for making jokes, and he nurtures his image of being "the president next door." His election campaign slogan was "come have a coffee with the president." While running for office, he traveled around the country chatting with people. They felt they could speak with him about any issue.

The president is elected by popular vote for a five-year term. Stjepan Mesic was elected president in 2000, and the country's next election is to be held in 2005. The prime minister, usually from the Parliament's majority party, is nominated by the president. Ivica Racan was prime minister from 2000 to 2003.

Restructuring Broad Powers

In 2000, Croatia's parliament voted to change the country's constitution to restrict the broad powers that were used by previous authoritarian presidents. Under the new constitution, the president continues to play a major role in determining defense and foreign policy. He also retains the power to dissolve the legislature, but only upon the request of the government, which includes the prime minister and the deputy ministers. The previous constitution allowed the president to dissolve Parliament single-handedly, to get rid of the prime minister, and to issue decrees with the force of law. The government now implements laws and handles the day-to-day running of modern Croatia.

Former prime minister Ivica Racan

The legislative branch of government consists of a unicameral, or one-house, parliament called the Sabor, which consists of 152 members. The representatives are elected by popular vote for four-year terms.

The National Assembly Building in Zagreb houses Croatia's parliament, the Sabor.

The Sabor was dissolved in October 2003, and elections were held that November to form a new Sabor. Croatian nationalists, most of whom belong to the Croatian Democratic Union (HDZ), took sixty-six seats in the voting and formed a new right-wing government. This dealt a blow to a reformist coalition that had held power in the preceding four years. The European Commission, which closely monitored the elections, said it would judge the new government on how it behaved before determining if it were ready to join the European Union in 2007. The HDZ allegedly encouraged violence during the war for independence from Yugoslavia in the 1990s. Under the party's direction, thousands of Serbs were forced to flee Croatia in 1995 in a brutal exodus.

Serbian refugees flee Croatia.

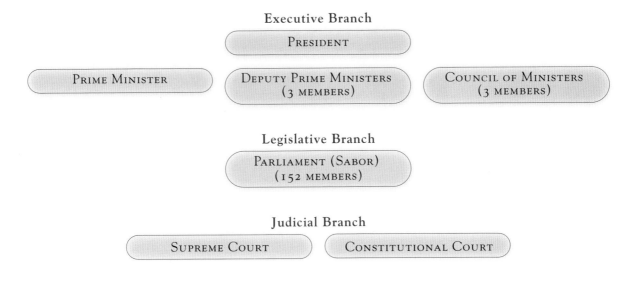

NATIONAL GOVERNMENT OF CROATIA

Executive Branch

PRESIDENT

PRIME MINISTER

DEPUTY PRIME MINISTERS
(3 MEMBERS)

COUNCIL OF MINISTERS
(3 MEMBERS)

Legislative Branch

PARLIAMENT (SABOR)
(152 MEMBERS)

Judicial Branch

SUPREME COURT

CONSTITUTIONAL COURT

Running for Office

Candidates from many political parties run for office and regularly form coalitions to increase their electoral power. The Croatian Christian Democratic Union, the Croatian Democratic Union, the Croatian People's Party, the Croatian Peasant Party, and the Croatian True Revival Party are among the numerous organizations that campaign fiercely for votes. Following the hard-fought elections in 2003, the Social Liberal Party (HSLS) and the HDZ formed a government under Ivo Sanader, the new prime minister. Sanader, a highly educated, skilled politician who speaks five languages, promised to set aside his party's often controversial nationalistic policies so that Croatia might be welcome in the European Union.

A Croatian woman casts her vote in the 2003 elections.

Croatians enjoy talking politics in coffee shops and on the street. Young people are encouraged to distribute fliers and otherwise take part in the country's vibrant political process. All Croatian citizens over the age of eighteen are eligible to vote. Anyone aged sixteen can also vote if employed full time. Women obtained the right to vote in 1946.

Judicial System

Judicial power is exercised by independent courts that administer justice according to the constitution and Croatian law. There are a total of 1,756 judges, and 1,084, or 62 percent, are women. There are 114 misdemeanor courts, 114 municipal courts, 13 commercial courts, 21 county courts, the High Misdemeanor Court, the High Commercial Court, and the Administrative Court. The highest judicial bodies are the Supreme Court and the Constitutional Court. Judges for each are appointed for eight-year terms by the Judicial Council of the Republic, which is elected by the Sabor.

National Anthem

The lyrics for the Croatian national anthem, "Our Beautiful Homeland" ("Lijepa nasa domovino"), were written by Antun Mihanovic (1796–1861). The lines first appeared in his poem, "Croatian Homeland," in the magazine *Morning Star* (*Danica*), on March 14, 1835. The musical score was composed in 1846 by Josip Runjanin (1821–1878), whose ancestry was Croatian Serb. The verses were first sung as the anthem in 1891.

Croatian version

Lijepa nasa domovino,
Oj junacka zemljo mila,
Stare slave djedovino,
Da bi vazda sretna bila!

Mila, kano si nam slavna,
Mila si nam ti jedina,
Mila, kuda si nam ravna,
Mila, kuda si planina!

Te cí, Dravo, Savo teci
Nit ti Dunav silu gubi,
Sinje more, svijetu reci:
Da svoj narod Hrvat ljubi.

Dok mu njive sunce grije,
Dok mu hrascé bura vije,
Dok mu mrtve grobak krije,
Dok mu zivo srce bije!

English version

Beautiful is our homeland,
Oh so fearless, oh so gracious,
Our fathers' ancient glory,
May God bless you, live forever!

Yes, you are our only glory,
Yes, you are our only treasure,
We love your plains and valleys,
We love your hills and mountains.

Sava, Drava, keep on flowing,
Danube, do not lose your vigor,
Deep blue sea go tell the whole world,
That a Croat loves his homeland.

When his fields are kissed by sunshine,
When his oaks are whipped by wild winds,
When his dear ones go to heaven,
Still his heart beats for Croatia!

The eleven-member Constitutional Court serves as a check on potential governmental attempts to circumvent, or get around, the spirit of the constitution. Among its important decisions, this court overruled a government interpretation of the conditions for citizenship by naturalization. This greatly increased the chances for Croatian Serb refugees to obtain citizenship. It also made a decision that strengthened the right to public assembly.

There are twenty-one political divisions in Croatia, made up of twenty counties called *zupanjie* (*zupanija* for a single county) and the single city (*grad*) of Zagreb. Local administrators govern Croatia's 120 towns and 146 communities. A number of town mayors have visited the United States to discuss common urban issues with the National League of Cities and the State Department.

Zagreb: Did You Know This?

With its population of 1,081,000 (2004), of which more than 75 percent is of Croatian heritage, Zagreb is Croatia's largest city. It has been the nation's capital since 1991. While people have lived in the area for many thousands of years, Slavic princes only began building forts and castles here in the A.D. 700s. In 1094 King Ladislav supported the establishment of the diocese of Zagreb.

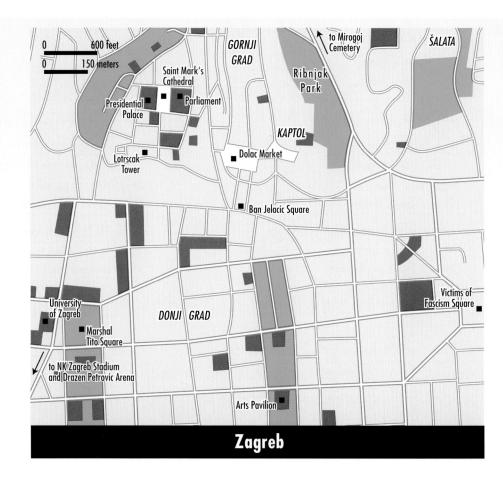

Zagreb

The city then began to expand. Zagreb was captured by the Mongols in 1242 and since then has been a great prize for other warring armies almost until modern times. Today, Zagreb is noted for its outdoor cafés and cultural life. The city is divided into three major sections: the thousand-year-old Upper Town, which contains the Presidential Palace and the Parliament; the nineteenth-century Lower Town, with numerous theaters and restaurants; and the New Town (Novi Zagreb) with an abundance of high-rise apartment buildings. The heart of the city is the central square, called Ban Jelacic Square. The city's average temperatures are 35°F (2°C) in January and 70°F (21° C) in July.

A Growing Economy

CROATIA IS STILL RECOVERING FROM THE ECONOMIC FAIL-ure of its Eastern European trading partners in the late 1980s. The collapse of the central government of Yugoslavia and the resulting war with Serbia in the 1990s also presented major challenges to the fragile Croatian economy. Although it had a fairly high standard of living after World War II, Croatia was hit hard by this triple punch. The war with Serbia alone cost an estimated $37 billion in damaged factories, wrecked roads, ruined hospitals, and leveled municipal buildings. In addition, there was the need to financially aid refugees from the war zones. At first, many refugees were unable to find work and housing and thus were an additional drain on the country's thin financial reserves.

The international community came to the rescue. Between 1994 and 2000, around $439.6 million was invested in Croatia by the European Bank for Reconstruction and Development and others. More assistance is needed, but many hesitant investors are

Opposite: **As Croatia's economy strengthens, many will have the opportunity to run their own businesses, including self-managed farms.**

A house is rebuilt after damage from war.

waiting until the region's political situation stabilizes before making large financial commitments.

Croatia was one of the most industrialized of the former Yugoslav republics. It emerged from its rural past in the days after World War II. Tens of thousands of people left the farms to seek work in the cities. Now, 57 percent of the population lives in Croatia's largest cities.

During the Communist era when many economic decisions were made by a centralized bureaucracy, Croatia's companies grew so big that they were inefficient and lost money. This was not a problem at that time because there was always a ready market for their goods. Now economists and potential investors say that such firms need to be privately owned and need to make a profit in order to survive in the global economy. Most Croatian business leaders are accepting that challenge. Today, there is a very advanced system of self-management in Croatia. There are about 60,000 individual firms in the country, and owners and workers want them to operate in a cost-effective manner. Some laborers, however, are upset about any proposed changes. They fear that their wages will drop. Many are also worried that they could lose their jobs as the country's business community rushes to rebuild and to modernize. Unemployment is high, hitting almost 23 percent in the early 2000s. There are 1.7 million workers in the country, with the average weekly wage less than $350. As a result, many young Croatians emigrate, looking for better job opportunities elsewhere. Most of them love their country and send money home.

Currency

Croatian money is based on the kuna, which replaced the Yugoslav dinar in 1994. In 2004, one American dollar was worth about 6.07 kuna. Kuna banknotes are issued in the following denominations: 5, 10, 20, 50, 100, 200, 500, and 1000. Kuna banknotes are very colorful. They are printed with the crest of the Republic of Croatia and the words of the national anthem on one side. Portraits of famous Croatian political and cultural leaders grace the other side. They are printed on cotton fiber, with metal security threads to prevent forgery.

The Croatian National Bank also issues coins in denominations of 1, 2, 5, 10, 20, and 50 lipa and 1, 2, 5, and 25 kuna. In addition to the year of minting, lipa coins have a picture of a leaf, and kuna coins feature a European marten, or weasel. The European euro and the United States dollar are also widely accepted throughout Croatia.

Croatia has major trading partners that seek goods. This is the Vegeta food products factory in Koprovnica.

Resources

Forests	Al Aluminum	Fe Iron ore
Mixed farming	Bx Bauxite	G Natural gas
Pasture livestock		
Vineyards	C Coal	Lg Lignite
Wheat and corn	Cem Cement	Petroleum

Producing Many Goods

Croatian factories produce textiles, fuel, processed food, lubricants, solvents, petrochemical products, and transportation equipment. Some industrial plants make quality waxes used for cleaning and for waterproofing wood products. Croatia's major trading partners today are Italy, Germany, Slovenia, Bosnia and Herzegovina, France, Russia, and Austria. Croatia often pairs with other countries to help with various development projects. For instance, to help increase the country's alternative energy output, German and Croatian partners have constructed wind "farms" at Pag, Novalja, and Oslije/Slano. A company from the United States and one from Turkey are working on a $990-million, 117-mile (188-km) toll road through the mountains. The job is especially dangerous because the workers have to carefully dispose of unexploded bombs and abandoned land mines remaining from Croatia's war with Yugoslavia. When finished, the road will link Zagreb to the coastal city of Split. Eventually, Dubrovnik will also be tied to the system. French companies are burrowing lengthy highway tunnels through the rugged landscape. Italian and Austrian companies are among other international firms working on construction projects in Croatia.

The Croatian shipbuilding industry has traditionally been an important contributor to the country's economy. The

Kraljevica Shipyard, established in 1729, is the nation's oldest. The Uljanik Shipyard began operations in 1852, and the Viktor Lena yard was launched in 1896. Business expanded after World War II, and Croatia became one of the world's top ship construction countries. They make new car ferries, oil and chemical tankers, container carriers, platforms for under-sea research, ocean tugs, and floating cranes and docks. There are also huge repair facilities that service large vessels from many other countries.

In the Korcula Shipyard, a Russian oil platform service boat is under construction.

Something "Fishy" in Croatia

For several years, oysters have been raised in the Adriatic Sea. This successful enterprise has encouraged another one. People of Croatian heritage living outside the country send money home to establish tuna farms. Since 1995, these hardy fish have been bred in submerged cages and have become world-famous for their flavor and quality. Up to 300 tons (305,088 kg) of fish a year are harvested in Croatia and sold primarily to Japan. This photo shows a crew emptying a cage filled with tuna.

Croatian farms are small family-run operations, averaging between 2 to 13 acres (1 to 5 ha). They raise a wide range of products. Wheat, corn, sugar beets, sunflower seeds, olives, fruit, soybeans, and potatoes are the major agricultural products.

Protecting Animals

Animal Friends Croatia, formed in 2001, is run by volunteers seeking to raise awareness of animal issues in their country. The association tries to ensure that the country's farm animals are treated humanely. The group also advocates not eating meat at all. Linked internationally via the Internet, the organization has received support from activists and vegetarians around the world who are also concerned about protecting animals. On one project, with the Croatian Ministry of Agriculture and Forestry, the group studied the problem of what to do with stray cats and dogs in the city of Zagreb. Animal Friends Croatia is also attempting to persuade the government to prohibit fishing with drift nets, dog fights, cosmetic experiments on animals, and similar challenges to the health and welfare of the animal world.

Stray cats and dogs are a concern in Croatia's cities. Organizations have been formed to protect these animals.

What Croatia Grows, Makes, and Mines	
Agriculture	
Corn	2,212,000 metric tons
Wheat	609,258 metric tons
Potatoes	553,700 metric tons
Manufacturing	
Clothing	24,399,000 metric tons
Linens	13,873,000 metric tons
Mining	
Natural gas	1,768,000 metric tons
Petroleum	1,214,000 metric tons

Tourists enjoy the sights of Old Town Alley in Split.

Weights and Measures

Croatia uses the metric system of weights and measures. Distances are measured in kilometers (1 kilometer equals 0.621 mile) and meters (1 meter is 3.2 feet). Weights include kilograms (1 kilogram is 2.2 pounds) and grams (1 gram equals 0.035 ounces).

Importance of Tourism

Tourism is a very important industry in Croatia. Almost 5 million international guests flock here each year to visit the many museums, art-packed galleries, ancient historical sites, exciting festivals, and other attractions. The warm, clean waters of the Adriatic are perfect for sailing, fishing, and snorkeling. Some visitors prefer simply loafing on the beautiful sandy beaches. Camping is a popular activity, especially on the offshore islands and land-based campsites near the sea. To keep their guests entertained, many camps have swimming pools, playgrounds, organized sports, horseback riding, mountaineering opportunities, tours, and workshops in such crafts as pottery and wood carving. Around 33 percent of all visitors to Croatia stay in campgrounds.

Croatians are hooked into the wide world. Everyone listens to the radio, where they get news, talk shows, and music on both AM and FM stations. There are an estimated 1.5 million radios in the country. The state radio-television monopoly is HRT, based at Zagreb. In addition, Austrian, Italian, and Slovenian radio and television broadcasts can be received. Radio 101 is a pioneer independent broadcast outlet also stationed in Croatia. In addition, Radio Rijeka is the first live Croatian radio channel on the Internet. The state-owned HTV carries three channels, commanding 95 percent of the

Workers of Radio 101 prepare for the day's broadcast.

There is no shortage of papers reporting current events in Croatia.

market. The daily newspaper, *Vjesnik*, is the most respected of the many Croatian language news publications, along with the Italian language *La Voce del Popolo*. Specialty periodicals such as *Nacional*, a political weekly published in Zagreb, are also widely read. News services like Croatia Net and HINA News Agency supply the latest background information and headlines on Croatian affairs to the world. With their 98.5 percent literacy rate, Croats are avid readers.

Communications and Transportation

The ringing of telephones can be heard all over Croatia. As elsewhere in the world, young Croatians love using the telephone to chat with their friends and to check in at home. There are more than 1.7 million phone lines in the country, and 1.3 million mobile phones. This sector of the communications industry is growing rapidly, with fashion-conscious users wanting the smallest and most stylish phones they can afford, just as they do elsewhere throughout the world. The nine Internet service providers are kept busy as more and more Croatians turn to computers for school, work, and home uses.

Croatia has an extensive transportation network, with 1,694 miles (2,726 km) of railroads carrying raw materials and finished goods to market. Passenger trains are usually efficient and clean. There are 17,404 miles (28,003 km) of highways, of which 14,723 miles (23,689 km) are paved. It is difficult to use the waterways, of which only 488 miles (785 km) are considered deep and wide enough to handle boats. Silt and other debris often clog the channels, blocking barges loaded with various goods. During the war with Serbia in the 1990s, many bridges were blown up or damaged on the Sava River. The wreckage is still being removed, and repairs are under way. This will open up more stretches of water to traffic.

Croatia's major ports bustle with merchant vessels from all over the world. Dubrovnik, Split, Zadar, Dugi Rat, Omisalj, Sibenik, Pula, Ploce, and Rijeka are the largest commercial facilities. Large, boxlike containers are loaded and unloaded at the port, sometimes piled four or five high in the storage yards, waiting to be moved. Inland, the port of Vukovar handles shipping on the Danube River.

Rijeka harbor is one of Croatia's main ports.

Croatia has forty-nine ships in its own transport fleet to haul bulk or refrigerated cargo, petroleum, and other materials.

There are sixty-seven airports in the country. Twenty-two of them can handle large passenger jets. Forty-five have only unpaved runways accommodating light planes. Many major international air carriers have passenger service to and from Croatia. Croatia's favorable geographic location in central Europe is excellent for business opportunities.

A Vibrant, Lively People

CROATIA'S POPULATION HAS BEEN ON A ROLLER COASTER ride for a decade. In 2003, there were 4,428,000 residents in the country, 78 percent of whom had Croatian heritage. More than 1 million Croats live in the other countries that made up the old Yugoslavia. Yet that figure has been bouncing up and down because of economic and political turmoil in the region. During the war with Serbia in the early 1990s, more than a quarter of a million Serbs who lived in Croatia feared for their lives and fled the country. Although the new Croatian constitution guarantees protection and equal rights for everyone, only a few of those Serbs returned to their old homes after the end of the fighting. Another quarter of a million Croatian refugees from battle-scarred Bosnia and Herzegovina flooded into Croatia. In addition, another 30,000 people escaped from the war-torn Vojvodina district of Serbia and made their way to Croatia. Only in Montenegro has the Croatian population has remained fairly stable.

Opposite: **Croats, proud of their heritage, perform at the Zagreb Folk Festival.**

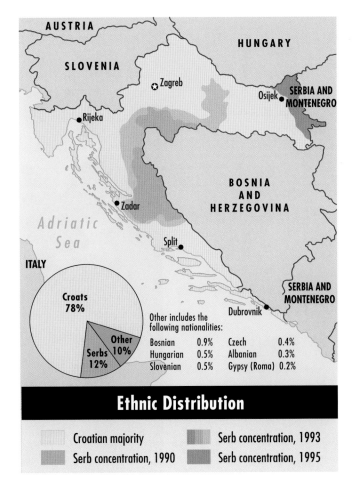

Ethnic Distribution

Croats 78%
Other 10%
Serbs 12%

Other includes the following nationalities:
Bosnian	0.9%	Czech	0.4%
Hungarian	0.5%	Albanian	0.3%
Slovenian	0.5%	Gypsy (Roma)	0.2%

Croatian majority
Serb concentration, 1990
Serb concentration, 1993
Serb concentration, 1995

Ethnic Breakdown of Croatia

Croat	78%
Serb	12%
Bosnian	1%
Hungarian	0.5%
Slovenian	0.5%
Czech	0.4%
Albanian	0.3%
Roma or Romany	0.2%
Other	7.1%

Croatian women live an average of seventy-eight years.

In addition to fleeing the horrors of war, some 130,000 Croats left their homeland over the past decade to search for better economic conditions. But this is nothing new. There was a great exodus in the late nineteenth century and again after World War II. It is estimated that about 2.3 million Croats now live outside their country. Of that figure, more than 1.5 million people in the United States have Croatian heritage. Pittsburgh, Pennsylvania, hosts one of the largest communities, numbering around 300,000. Another 270,000 Croats live in Germany; 150,000 reside in Canada; and 150,000 have found new homes in Argentina.

Of the entire population remaining in the country, 18.3 percent are under fourteen years old. That breaks down into 411,847 boys and 390,797 girls. The bulk of the people, 66.3 percent, are between fifteen and sixty-four years old. The average life span of a Croatian is seventy-four years, with women living to around seventy-eight years old and men making it to seventy. The average family has two children.

Croatian as First Language

Ninety-six percent of the people speak Croatian as their first language, and another 4 percent speak Italian, Hungarian, Czech, Slovak, or German as their native tongue. In addition, almost all Croats speak at least one other language, because they live in a crossroads area with numerous ethnic heritages. Often they are fluent in three or four languages, including English. Young people learn English in the lower grades, and a number of advanced students attend the American International School in Zagreb. In addition to the Croatian staff, teachers from Winnipeg, Canada; Paris, France; and Carolina Beach, North Carolina, teach at the international school.

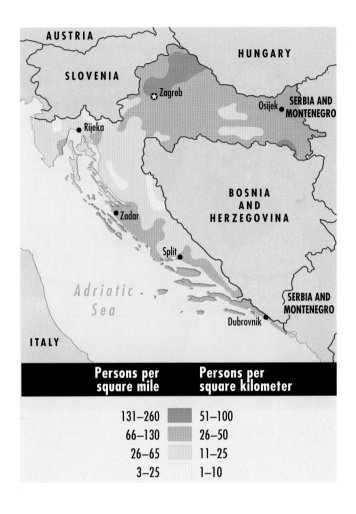

Persons per square mile	Persons per square kilometer
131–260	51–100
66–130	26–50
26–65	11–25
3–25	1–10

Population of Croatia's Largest Cities (2004 est.)

Zagreb	1,081,000
Split	172,700
Rijeka	141,800

A welcome sign in Zagreb

Speaking Croatian

There are thirty letters in the Croatian alphabet. Five are vowel sounds, and the rest are consonants. Some of the letters are diacritical, which means they have accent marks above them. Such marks are not used in English. Although Serbian and Croatian are two separate languages, the term *Serbo-Croatian* was used to describe their languages throughout the history of the former country of Yugoslavia. This was an artificial attempt to forge these two different Slavic peoples into a single nation. Today, language experts no longer use that description and note the distinct qualities of each.

Common Croatian Words and Phrases

zdravo	hello
dovidenja	good-bye
da	yes
ne	no
molim	please
hvala	thank you
Govorite li engleski?	Do you speak English?
Kako ti je ime?	What's your name?
Moje ime je ...	My name is ...
Odakle ste?	Where are you from?
Ja sam iz Kanade.	I am from Canada.
Ja sam iz Amerike.	I am from the United States.

Ties with Western Europe

Unlike some of its neighbors, such as the Bosnians or Serbs, Croatians have traditionally strong but often stormy ties with Western Europe. Historically, anyone traveling beyond Croatia would be venturing into the "East," where the ancient Ottoman Empire ruled long ago from its base in Turkey. Croatians have always been proud to have been called the bulwark of the West against invasions by fierce warriors from the East, whether they were Tartars, Mongols, or Turks. Croatian armies have fought many battles over the years for independence and to preserve their heritage. Various parts of their traditional territory regularly fell under the control of such outsiders as the Venetians, French, Austrians, and Hungarians, so they kept their Western heritage, rather than that of Eastern cultures.

Croatian young people are well aware of their history. They need only look out their windows to see the past, whether they live in the industrial center of Cakovec or the farming village of Belec. Youngsters are surrounded by churches, monasteries, fortresses, statues, fountains, plazas, and streets that whisper of the old days. Yet their schooling takes them confidently forward.

Kids in School

Croatian children attend public kindergarten, then go to an elementary school for the first through eighth grades. After the primary grades comes high school and then college. Class sizes vary in Croatian schools, but the average is twenty-five pupils per room, which is about the same as in Canada and the United States. As in North America, there are more women than men teaching school.

School children on an outing in Split

In the lower grades there is one teacher for all the subjects. In grade five, schoolchildren start moving to different classrooms for history, science, mathematics, and other lessons. When there is a class break, hallways are filled with laughing, joking, and shouting kids. But when the teacher is ready to start, everyone becomes serious. Favorite classes are art, biology, and music. Croatian children often take top honors in international competitions for mathematics and science. After school, many children are on a sports team or involved in a club, choir, or other extracurricular fun. Homework comes after that.

A high-school student carves a fountain in a sculpture workshop.

Arts are considered very important in Croatia and are included in the school curriculum. Music, drawing and printing, dance, modeling, creative writing, and history of art are taught throughout primary and secondary schools. Professional artists help the teachers with exciting projects and extra classes. Funding for such programs comes from the Ministry of Education and Sport, which is responsible for all teachers' salaries and the maintenance of school buildings. Parents, town councils, and civic groups pay for some of the optional programs that might involve field trips or other extra costs.

Croatian children, especially those in rural areas where fighting raged in the early 1990s, need to be aware of leftover bombs and unexploded land mines. The government has launched a project with leaflets and videos warning youngsters of these dangers. When a bomb is found, young people are taught not to go near it and to notify the authorities so no one will be hurt. Many schools also offer special help to displaced and refugee children, as well as assisting their parents in adjusting to a different life in a new place. Getting used to a new home can be very scary. Teachers and school counselors help to make the transition easier for children who may have had to escape from enemy soldiers.

Love of Outdoors

Youngsters who love the outdoors eagerly take advantage of an Eco-Schools program that started in Croatia in 1998. The project was modeled after the Keep Britain Tidy project, which also helps kids to learn how to care for their environment. The Croatian Youth Hostel Association also encourages young Croatians to hike, swim, and enjoy other outside activities during the summer or on trips outside the classroom.

Children enjoy the cool, calm, clear waters of Croatia's coast.

After four years of high school, students can enter the workforce or go on for more studies. Learning has a long and distinguished history in Croatia, and a scholar is highly respected. Higher education in Croatia dates back to 1396 when the Dominicans, a Roman Catholic order of priests, established a school called the Universitas Jadertina in Zadar. This was the first university in Croatia to confer degrees and was equal in status to major universities elsewhere in Europe at the time.

Today, Croatia has four major universities, which are located at Zagreb, Rijeka, Split, and Osijek. Seven polytechnic schools emphasize the sciences and engineering. In addition, there are six independent schools of professional higher education, one teachers' academy, and eight teachers' schools. Undergraduate study spans at least four years. Young people in undergraduate professional studies need at least two years in order to receive an associate degree. To help students requiring financial assistance, the Croatian Scholarship Fund was established in late 1989 by Croatian Americans living in the San Francisco Bay Area.

Among the Croatian specialty schools is the American College of Management and Technology in Dubrovnik. This institution was founded in 1997 with the help of the Rochester Institute of Technology in the United States. More than 700 students prepare for business careers at this school. Today, the college is the only private educational institution in Croatia awarding both American and Croatian degrees.

To broaden their view of the world, students are encouraged to attend schools in other countries or to participate in study visits outside the country. Many professors are active in joint scientific research projects with colleagues around the world. As a result, young Croatians are becoming much better prepared to lead their nation into the future.

CHAPTER

EIGHT

Church
and Faith

86

ELASCICA IS A LARGE COVE ON THE SOUTH END OF DUGI Otok Island. Steep cliffs rearing up from the roaring sea lend a mysterious aura to the place. According to local myths, ancient seafarers buried gold on the island. And there are legends of strange little people who live there, all of them having five small horns sprouting from their heads.

Visitors to Croatia probably won't see these fabled creatures, but there are plenty of churches and other religious sites to tour. Early people living in what is now Croatia first worshipped nature, but as time went on, they gradually adopted a series of gods. The most popular early deity was Silvanus, who probably originated as the fun-loving Greek god Pan. This creature was supposedly half man and half goat. On bits and pieces of pots and other artifacts found by archaeologists, Silvanus was always depicted with three wood nymphs holding hands. These were beautiful young women who took care of the major deities. Some of the gods of the Illyrians, an ancient race of people who once lived in Croatia, were absorbed

Opposite: **Saint Stephen's Cathedral in Zagreb**

Croatia's favored god was Silvanus, similar to the Greek god Pan as seen below.

by the Romans and given new names. For instance, the Illyrians' Thana became Diana, and Iria evolved into Venus.

In 1999, an archaeological team from Canada's Royal Ontario Museum discovered the Nakovana Cave on the southern Dalmatian coast. It was hiding an altar and fertility symbols dating from the days of the Illyrians. Numerous burial sites of Illyrian warriors were found nearby. Researchers have learned a great deal about this ancient culture by studying the broken pots and other artifacts discovered in the cavern, sealed off for more than 2,000 years. Nakovana is considered one of the most important ancient sites on the Adriatic. Place names such as Crkvina, from the Croatian *crkva* meaning "church," indicate that this city was also a long-ago religious site. Early Asian religions also made a brief appearance in Croatia, such as the followers of Mithraism who worshipped the sun.

Missionaries Come to Croatia

Christian missionaries made their way across Croatia as early as A.D. 100. Congregations were soon established and bishops appointed. By the 400 and 500s, Christianity was widely accepted, and it became the official state religion early in the 800s. Followers of the early missionaries celebrated mass in the local Slavic languages, in addition to the more widely accepted Latin common to Roman Catholic liturgies elsewhere. Slavic writing evolved into what is known as the Glagolitic alphabet. In 1248, the Croats were given permission by Pope Innocent IV to use their own language and this style of writing in their liturgies. At the time, they were the only Europeans granted this special privilege. Even today, some Croatian churches still use texts written in Glagolitic script.

Pagan temples usually were torn down and Christian churches erected on their sites. These small structures were often built in the shape of a cross, to remind worshippers how Christ died. Only a few of Croatia's early religious buildings remain intact. Sveti Kriz, the Church of the Holy Cross in Nin, near Zadar, is only thirty-six steps across. Yet despite its tiny size, the building is one of the most historically significant structures in Croatia. The dimensions of the church were set according to the position of the sun, which meant the building was a clock and a calendar, as well as a place of worship. Dating from the early 800s, Sveti Kriz was probably the seat of

Early missionaries traveled to Slavic lands converting early peoples to Christianity.

Tiled roof of Saint Mark's church

power for a local bishop. Above a doorway is an inscription indicating that the church was founded by Prince Godezav. This is the earliest known reference to any Croatian ruler over the country's long history.

Tourists can still see Saint Krsevan's on the road to Krk and the Church of the Holy Trinity in Poljud near Split. These are excellent examples of early houses of worship. Larger, more elaborate basilicas were built in the 1000s and 1100s. One of the most beautiful is Saint Mark's Church in the medieval Upper Town (*gornji grad*) of Zagreb, a structure that dates to the 1200s. Even its roof has multicolored tiles arranged in intricate patterns. Regardless of their size, the church buildings were always vividly painted and contained marvelous frescoes, paintings, and sculptures, mostly of religious themes.

By studying this evolving architecture, youngsters get a better understanding of the past. Because religion, culture, and politics became so entwined over the years, students can recognize how their Croatian world has changed over the centuries.

Zagreb's Cathedral

The history of Zagreb centers around the huge Cathedral of the Assumption of the Blessed Virgin. Many twin spires soar 344 feet (105 m) above the city, making it easy to find. Built on the ruins of an earlier church, the cathedral was destroyed by the Tatars in 1242. Rebuilt, it was damaged by fires, earthquakes, and war many times. The look of the current building dates from the end of World War II, with a remnant of an old fortification still visible on the eastern side. Among the many artworks in the building are 500 paintings and more than 300 sculptures, as well as exhibits of valuable clerical attire worn over the centuries. The image shown is of the Grand Altar, made of sculpted wood. The church houses the tomb of Croatia's saintly Cardinal Alojzije Stepinac. His strong voice spoke out for the rights of the people during the fascist and Communist eras of the 1940s through the 1960s.

A Churchgoing People

The majority of Croats are Roman Catholics, while Serbs living in the country are mostly Eastern Orthodox. There are a few Muslims and Jews and a very small number of Protestants.

These religions are about the only elements separating residents of the country. For all outward appearances, everyone looks and dresses the same. The roots of the Roman and Orthodox split go back to the waning days of the Roman Empire. Among their doctrinal differences, Roman Catholics do not allow their priests to marry, and they follow the leadership of the pope, who lives in Vatican City in Rome, Italy. On the other hand, Orthodox clergy may have wives and are not under the pope's authority.

Catholicism is a basic factor of life in Croatia, where nearly all social life revolves around the church. Croatians became Christians in the A.D. 800s and have been loyal to their faith ever since. Over the generations Croatian kings built great cathedrals and maintained monasteries in support of their religion.

Young adults pray in Zagreb's Saint Catherine church.

Over the incredibly long years when Croatian life was under the thumb of outsiders, the Catholic faith unified the people. It gave them a purpose to continue their struggle for freedom. Under the fascists of the World War II era, however, this religious fervor was misdirected into allowing attacks on Jews and other minorities. After the war, the Communist regime of Yugoslavia allowed religion to be practiced, although it wasn't openly supported. Subsequently, the churches remained hotbeds of nationalist enthusiasm. This contributed to the breakup of Yogoslavia in the 1990s, as the Orthodox states went in one direction and Roman Catholic Croatia turned another way. Under the rule of Franjo Tudjman, the first president after the breakaway from Yugoslavia, the church's role was solidified. Schools were required to offer religion classes, but children were not obliged to take them. Church property confiscated by the Communists was returned. The government financially supported church activities. In exchange, the Vatican allowed civil marriages to be just as legal as weddings by priests.

Cardinal Josip Bozanic was outspoken regarding the intentions of the Tudjman government.

Monitoring the Government

This cozy church-state relationship was not always very friendly. Some clergy objected to the government prosecution of accused Catholic war criminals from World War II, which set them at odds with the rest of the international community. Some clergy also supported the resettlement of Orthodox Serbs during the 1990s war and were glad to have refugee Croatian Catholics replace them. Another instance of discord was that Cardinal Josip Bozanic of Zagreb often protested corruption in the Tudjman government. This helped lead to new elections in 2000.

Croatia's Book of Miracles

The large, leather-bound *Book of Miracles* is secreted away in the Franciscan Church in Klostar Ivanic, a building dating from 1719. The volume was compiled between 1757 and 1782 in the local Kajkavian dialect. Each story relates a miracle that happened to someone living in the area. Diseases were reportedly cured, and other wondrous things happened to believers who prayed in front of a portrait of the Blessed Virgin Mary, the mother of Jesus.

The city celebrates its religious heritage on June 24, the birthday of John the Baptist. This fair started in the 1500s and includes exhibitions by high-stepping horses pulling beautifully decorated carts.

Klostar Ivanic also has processions on the feast of the Assumption each August 15 and holds church services on Saint Nicholas Day in December and on Christmas. The patrons of wine and winemakers, Saints Vincent and Martin, also hold a special place in the hearts of churchgoers who live in the town. Croatia is known for its excellent wine and fun wine festivals.

Although most Croatians consider themselves to be very religious, only about 30 percent attend church services regularly. However, the clergy still has a respected position in Croatian society.

Christmas Fun

Christmas is a favorite time of year, and celebrating is a time for families to gather, attend church, eat big meals, and sometimes distribute gifts. Saying "*Sretan Bozic*," or "Merry Christmas," is a cheery holiday greeting. On Christmas Eve, fish is eaten instead of meat, along with *badnji kruh*, a bread made with honey, nuts, and dried fruit. On the Dalmatian coast, the fish is traditionally dried, salted cod called *bakalar*. For Christmas dinner, the main course might be roast suckling pig, a whole turkey, or roast beef, depending on the region. On Christmas Day, a sweet-smelling glazed bread packed with nutmeg, raisins, and almonds is braided into the shape of a

Croatia's Religions

Roman Catholic	76%
Orthodox	11%
Muslim	1.2%
Protestant	0.4%
Other	11.4%

wreath. Candles are placed in the center of the loaf, which is used as a centerpiece for Christmas dinner. The bread is left on the table until the Feast of the Epiphany on January 6, when it is cut and eaten. According to tradition, this is the day that the Three Wise Men (also called the Three Kings) visited the infant Jesus in Bethlehem.

Although gifts are sometimes exchanged on Christmas Day, this is not the main gift-giving time for Croatian youngsters. They also receive presents on special saints' days. In southern and northeastern Croatia, children can barely wait until December 13, when Saint Lucy brings her gifts. In northern and central Croatia, Saint Nicholas arrives with goodies on December 6. Youngsters prepare for the holiday by hopefully placing their shoes on the floor beside their beds. The shoes are then filled with treats by the good saint. (Actually, the parents tiptoe quietly into the bedrooms after the children are asleep in order to leave goodies.)

Santa Claus drives his Christmas tram through the streets of Zagreb.

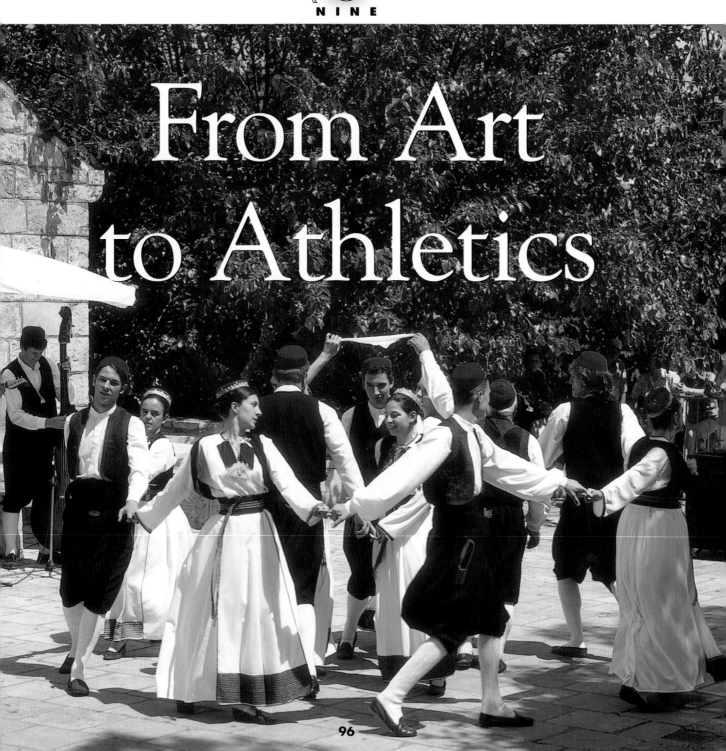

From Art
to Athletics

W

ITH HUNDREDS OF YEARS OF HISTORY BEHIND IT, IT IS no wonder that Croatia has an extensive lineup of marvelous writers, painters, musicians, actors, and sports figures.

Opposite: **Traditional folk performers dance to the tunes of folk musicians.**

Architecture and Art

Reaching far into its past, Croatia can point proudly to church architect Juraj Dalmatinac (George of Dalmatia) who lived between 1420 and 1473. He is considered to be the first builder ever to put together individual parts of a building, haul them to a construction site, then assemble the pieces like a puzzle. Among his most notable structures is the Saint James Cathedral, on the main square in Sibenik. In an ornate band

As on the Saint James Cathedral, sculpted heads adorn the wall of the Sibenik Cathedral. Peasants to villains of the 1400s are portrayed.

From Art to Athletics **97**

around the walls are the likenesses of seventy-one individuals, important people from those days whose heads seem frozen into the intricately carved stonework. The cathedral took almost a century to complete. Its dome was so carefully constructed that it has never leaked in more than five hundred years!

Master Radovan was a widely appreciated medieval sculptor. One of his most famous works is the portal of the Cathedral of Saint Lovro (Lawrence). The church is in the lovely seaport of Trogir, an historic community on the UNESCO World Heritage list. It had been colonized by Greeks in the fourth century B.C. In 1240, Radovan sculpted several scenes highlighting Christ's birth, including the travels of the Three Kings and the worshipping by the shepherds. He also depicted Adam and Eve, becoming the first European to carve the two biblical figures as contemporary characters. Art lovers from around the world flock to Trogir to admire his creations.

Supporter of the Arts

Among all the supporters of the arts in Croatia, few have the stature of Bishop Josip Juraj Strossmajer (1815–1905) of Djakovo. In 1861, the clergyman helped found the Croatian Academy of Sciences and Arts, dedicated to the study of the country's history, culture, languages, and heritage. Its status as an academic institution was formalized five years later by Francis Joseph I, emperor of Austria and king of Hungary. For many years, the bishop collected art, ranging from fifteenth-century Italian primitives to contemporary Croatian painters.

In 1868, Bishop Strossmajer donated his collection to the Croatian people, to be placed under the protection of the academy. The works were housed in a palace in Zagreb. The gallery and the palace opened to the public in 1884, with 256 marvelous pieces. Many other important artworks have been added to the internationally respected collection. A firm believer in the importance of education, Strossmajer helped found the modern University of Zagreb, in 1874, with an emphasis on science, engineering, law, theology, and philosophy.

Trogir is the home to many of Radovan's sculptures.

Another Croatian sculptor, Ivan Mestrovic (1883–1962), was famous for his larger-than-life statues of ancient Croat and Slavic folk heroes and of American Indians. Many of his works can be found in Chicago, Illinois. Mestrovic traveled all over Europe and regularly visited North America, becoming a United States citizen in 1954.

Ivan Mestrovic is famous for his sculptures of folk heroes. This is Gregorius of Nin.

The Greatest Naive Artist

Artist Ivan Generalic (1914–1992) is considered one of Croatia's greatest painters. He grew up in the farm village of Hlebine, and became a cowherd. Even as a youngster, Generalic carried pencils and chalk with him to make pictures of whatever he saw all around. Sometimes he just used a sharp stick to draw in the ground. When other workers took rest breaks, Generalic created scenes of animals and farm life. When he was older, the artist painted what he remembered from his rural childhood. Generalic eventually moved to Zagreb and then to Paris, where he became exposed to a broader art world, yet he kept his own naïve, or unschooled, style that was greatly admired.

One of his most famous works is the vibrant, bustling *Cattle Fair*, painted in 1971. It is only one of his many colorful paintings depicting harvesting, wine making, and other day-to-day life in rural Croatia. Generalic returned to live near his home village in 1975, where he continued to paint. The featured painting below is Generalic's *Rest at Noon Time*.

His simple style, depicting ordinary people at their jobs, prompted numerous young artists to follow his example. One of Generalic's famous students was rustic painter Dragan Gazi (1930–1983), who was also born in Hlebine. Gazi often depicted countryside scenes, using oil paint on glass.

The early Croatian artists who primarily decorated the walls of churches were rarely identified by name. Only in the 1300s did individual artists become known for their work. Among the most prominent painters of that era were Blaz Jurjev Trogiranin (?–1448), Juraj Culinovic (1433–1503), and Nikola Bozidarevic (1460–1517). The Croatian Art Society, was founded in 1878, helped make Zagreb one of central Europe's major cultural centers. Throughout the 1880s and 1890s, a "Zagreb school" of painting, featuring rich colors and realistic details, was led by Vlaho Bukovac (1855–1922). He made his way to Paris, France, and became very successful financially. His followers usually painted portraits of ordinary people, as well as village scenes, folklife, and quiet country scenes.

The 1920s saw another flowering of Croatian art, especially with portrayals of peasant life. After World War II, a number of Croatian artists went elsewhere to live, taking their talents to share with the world. Kristian Krekovic (1901–1985), for example, moved to Peru and produced huge paintings of Inca Indians and their mountain landscapes. Two contemporary painters, Nives Kavuric-Kurtovic (1938–) and Vatrolslav Kulis (1951–), approach their subjects in more abstract ways.

Loving the Words

Croats adore words, how they sound and how they fit into a story. They are noted for their wonderful folktales, thought-provoking novels, and humorous short stories. Literature truly flowered in the 1400 and 1500s, even though Croatia was ruled by outsiders. Their lack of political independence encouraged writers to work doubly hard to preserve the language and heritage of their ancestors. One such author was Ivan (Dzivo) Gundulic (1589–1638), a poet whose epic poem *Osman* celebrated Croatia's freedom-loving spirit. Yet all the writing was not necessarily serious. The poet Sisko Mencetic (1457–1527) is remembered for writing short lyric verses about his many girlfriends. Marin Drzic (1508–1567) was Europe's best comedy writer during the Renaissance. Experts consider him a forerunner of Shakespeare.

Writing for the Young

There are several contemporary children's authors whose stories delight kids throughout Europe. Zlata Kolaric-Kisur (1894–1990) began writing children's poetry as a way of providing reading material for her daughter. An anthology, or

Croatia's Beloved Krleza

Zagreb native Miroslav Krleza (1893–1981) was one of Croatia's best-loved authors. He wrote numerous essays, poems, novels, and plays that have been translated into dozens of languages. Krleza's most ambitious work was the six-volume *Zastave*, completed in 1967. The story was a sweeping overview of European life between 1912 and 1922. In 1993, on the 100th anniversary of his birth, Krleza was honored by a stamp with his likeness, drawn by artist Marija Ujevic.

Krleza became a common soldier during World War I, but his experiences in the trenches caused him to hate war. Throughout his life Krleza fearlessly defended his views against what he saw as stupidity in the government and upper classes. Krleza disliked all forms of dictatorship and remained a supporter of Croatian nationalism. He influenced an entire generation of young Croatian writers who came after him. Krleza's essays criticizing Yugoslavia's politicians, and the staging of his plays in the Croatian National Theater, were admired by the country's liberals, who found support and comfort in his brave words.

collection, of her materials was published in 1994 on the 100th anniversary of her birth. She is considered the bridge between traditional and modern Croatian children's poets. Stanislav Feminic (1924–) is another notable children's author whose books include *Fear in the Forest* and funny little poems like "The Angry Cowboy." Ratko Zvrko (1920–1998) had several careers in addition to writing for youngsters. He was a journalist for a daily newspaper and a middleweight boxing champion when he was young.

Delightful stories by Ivana Brlic-Mazuranic (1874–1938) are read by almost every Croatian youngster. Her words captured the innocence of kids, who could readily identify with her characters. Her *Tales of Long Ago* was translated into many other languages. With this book and other writings, Brlic-Mazuranic stimulated interest in the fairytales and folk

Winning the Nobel Prize

Serbo-Croatian author Ivo Andric (1892–1975) won the Nobel Prize in literature in 1961. Born a Croat in a Catholic enclave of Muslim Bosnia, Andric received his award for an historical trilogy called *The Bridge on the Drina*, *Bosnian Story*, and *Young Miss*. Although he was from Bosnia, Andric published his first works in Zagreb and considered himself a Yugoslav. He also lived in Belgrade, where his books were published in Serbian. Andric's stories are now being used in Croatian schools as examples of excellent native writing.

legends of the ancient Croats. The world appreciated her compositions, too, and she was nominated for the Nobel Prize in literature in 1931 and 1938. Highly respected at home, she was the first woman accepted into the Croatian Academy of Sciences and Arts, in 1937. A coin issued by the Croatian National Bank bears her likeness.

Croatians appreciate all forms of music from local musicians to popular rock bands.

Croatian Music

While early Croatian music consists primarily of folk songs and hymns for church services, the country has a long list of classical composers. In the 1700s, Luka Sorkocevic of Dubrovnik produced eight symphonies, and Ivan Padovec wrote a number of exciting guitar compositions. Vatroslav Lisinksi (1819–1854) mixed music and writing when he created Croatia's first opera, *Love and Malice*, in 1846.

An appreciation of excellent music is still evident. A national contest of marching bands is a popular annual event, with competing groups playing everything from Latino music

An audience enjoys an opera performance in the courtyard of the Palace of Diocletian.

to rock. Today, of course, rock music is "in," as it is throughout the world. In the larger cities, narrow alleyways lead to crowded nightclubs where bands like the Misfits and Slayer perform to packed houses. Many girls cut their hair short, dyeing it deep black or layering their locks in crazy, rainbow colors. Guys with shaved heads and pierced ears stand around in leather jackets, listening to the pulsating sounds.

Yet classical music, particularly operas, remain favorites with Croatian audiences. Ivan Zajc (1832–1914) composed more than one thousand pieces of music, including masses and oratorios. He is favorably compared with such famous composers as Verdi. Zajc's *Nikola Subic Zrinski* is an important part of the repertoire of the Zagreb Opera House. Jakov Gotovac

(1895–1982) composed the Croatian opera *Ero from Another World*, a soaring piece of music that is still performed on the world's stages. Many Croatian musicians have become famous conductors, violinists, singers, and other important artists with major international orchestras.

Noted Pianist

Ivo Pogorelich is one of Croatia's best-known classical musicians. The award-winning pianist was born in 1958 in Belgrade. He started his musical education at the age of seven. When he was twelve his family moved to Moscow, where he studied at the Central School of Music and the Tchaikovsky Conservatory. In 1980, he gained international attention by capturing the first prize in the prestigious International Music Competition at Montreal, Canada. Pogorelich has performed in New York's Carnegie Hall and throughout Europe, Australia, Japan, South America, and Israel. He gives about eighty concerts a year, often for charities. His recorded music is always a best seller.

Pogorelich established the Young Musicians' Fellowship in 1986 to help budding Croatian musicians with living expenses. In 1994, he founded the Sarajevo Charitable Foundation to raise money for a hospital to serve mothers and children. UNESCO has honored him as one of its worldwide ambassadors of goodwill, the first classical musician to be so appointed.

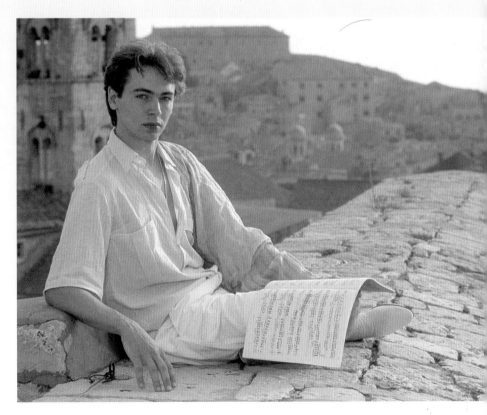

The beat of electronic music is known worldwide, as evidenced by Mitar Subotic (1961–1999), nicknamed Suba. He was a Croatian-born record producer who lived in Paris and São Paulo, Brazil. An ardent follower of Afro-Brazilian rhythm, Indian music, and jazz, Suba blended his own central European heritage into global themes. Suba tragically died in a fire in his studio in 1999 while trying to save original recordings of a friend's new album.

Also popular on the world's stages is award-winning Matija Dedic, born in Zagreb in 1973. As a youngster, he attended the primary and high schools of music arts in the Croatian capital. Dedic frequently appears on television and in concerts. His mother, Gabi Novak, is a famous Croatian singer who often accompanied the gravelly-voiced Louis Armstrong, the famous African American jazz trumpeter. Dedic's father, Arsen, is a well-known Croatian singer and songwriter.

Theater Scene

Croatian theater traditionally featured splashy, romantic productions about brave folk heroes. Because the country was ruled by outsiders for so long, these plays kept alive a sense of national identity. Because of the political nature of these pieces, they were criticized and often banned by the authorities. Yet the words kept flowing, and actors kept acting. Playwrights of the last half of the nineteenth century included Mirko Bogovic, Ljudevit Vukotinovic, and Hugo Badalic. Around World War I, the works of Milan Ogrizovic, Higin Dragosic, and Tito Strozzi were popular among the Croatians,

if not with their Habsburg rulers. In the late 1960s, Ivan Raos and Nicola Sop restaged some of the classics from the previous century to great acclaim. Among contemporary playwrights are Vladimir Stojsavljevic and Milan Ogrizovic, who have taken advantage of Croatia's new nationhood to write much more freely.

Dramatic performances are staged at the Croatian National Theatre in Zagreb.

Movie Making

The first movie ever shown in Croatia was an unnamed film that ran in 1896 in Zagreb's Kolo Hall. The country's first studio, Croatia, started in 1917, the same year that a motion picture school began in Zagreb, making it one of the world's first. The nation's first notable director at Croatia was Arnost Grund (1866–1929). Movies have been made in Croatia ever since those early days. The Zagreb cartoon school was internationally known between 1957 and 1968, and the nation's golden age of filmmaking occurred early in the 1970s. Two famous movies from that era were Kristo Papic's *Lisice* (*Foxes*) and *Bablje ljeto* (*Indian Summer*) by Nikola Tanhofer. However, some film producers and directors were imprisoned for their liberal political beliefs as that decade wore on. This dampened enthusiasm for making movies in Croatia, and it took more than a decade for the industry to recover. Croatian movies are again being shown at major international film festivals.

Many young people now join drama clubs, and almost every Croatian school has an auditorium or theater where plays are presented to much applause. Since the late 1960s, the coastal town of Sibenik has hosted the International Children's Festival. The fifteen-day event draws about 950 participants from Croatia, Japan, Brazil, Poland, Cameroon, France, Bosnia and Herzegovina, and Slovenia. Participants perform in more than one hundred programs and take part in theatrical workshops.

Croatian theaters regularly show American movies, as well as films from other countries. Just as in Canada and the United States, kids eagerly await the latest adventures of Harry Potter, Frodo Baggins, or the antics of Jim Carrey. The local theater is a popular place for youngsters to gather.

Sports

Sports are integral to the day-to-day life of Croatia. The country's mountains are a challenge for cliff climbers and hikers,

Cycling across Croatia's countryside is a popular outdoor sport.

Croatian "snow queen" Janica Kostelic celebrates victory in Zagreb's main square after winning three gold medals at the 2002 Winter Olympics.

and its clear offshore waters are perfect for sailing and fishing. In addition to many amateur sports opportunities, Croatians have competed in Olympic events over the years. In the 2000 summer games, weightlifter Nikolay Pechaliv won a gold medal in the men's featherweight division. The country's eight-man rowing team captured a bronze. After the 2002 winter games, almost 100,000 people flooded Zagreb's main square to welcome Croatia's Olympic triple-gold medalist Janica Kostelic (1982–). Nicknamed "Janica the Snow Queen," the twenty-year-old Zagreb resident was the first woman to take three alpine skiing gold medals at a single Winter Olympics. She also won a silver medal in a fourth event.

Soccer is Croatia's national sport. Young fans keep devoted track of their sports heroes in magazines and newspapers, as well as on television. Schools have teams, and just about every town in the country has a soccer club. NK Zagreb is the largest team in the capital city, with a fancy Web site and internationally ranked players. Split's clubs, such as Jadran Hajduk (The Bandit), play in Poljud Stadium, considered to be one of the country's best athletic facilities. Croatia's national team has played twice in the World Cup. It captured a third place in 1998 and played again in 2002, but was defeated in the initial rounds.

Players love mingling with their fans, and many take on charitable causes to support them. Zvone Boban, the legendary captain of the Croatian national team, was a sports

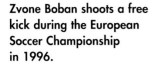

Zvone Boban shoots a free kick during the European Soccer Championship in 1996.

Slamming the Ball

Croatia has a love affair with handball. It became the Olympic handball champion in 1996 and won its first World Cup championship handball title in 2003. Led by coach Lino Cervar, the Croatians pulled a surprise victory by beating Germany in the finals, 34 to 31. To earn its place in the competition, Croatia's national team had defeated rival Spain, 39 to 37, in two fiercely fought overtime matches played in Portugal.

ambassador for the SOS Childen's Village Croatia. When he retired at age thirty-four in 2002, he treated all the SOS kids with tickets to his final match in Maksimir Stadium in Zagreb in front of 40,000 cheering fans. Funds raised at that game went toward constructing an SOS Youth Community in Osijek, providing housing for fourteen high school students. The SOS project provides safe haven for young people displaced by war or economic challenges at home.

Mario Ancic

Croats do well in other sports, too. In 2001, Goran Ivanisevic became the first Croat to win at Wimbledon, England, the world's most prestigious tennis tournament. Ivanisevic was born in Split, and started to play tennis at age seven. He went professional in 1988, when he was only seventeen. After he defeated Australian Patrick Rafter, Ivanisevic said he hoped he was not going to wake up from what seemed like a dream. Another up-and-coming tennis star is young Mario Ancic. Both tennis stars live in Split and are good friends despite their age difference, often playing doubles together. Born in 1984, Ancic studies law and enjoys touring art studios and galleries when he travels to competitions in Australia, Britain, and elsewhere.

Slam, Dunk, and Score

The National Basketball Association is glad to have a player like Toni Kukoc (right, in purple) of Split, who is a fast-driving forward with the Milwaukee Bucks. Born in 1968, Kukoc decided to play basketball in a roundabout way. As a youngster, he was Croatian national champion in table tennis. He then played soccer. He was fifteen years old before he even thought about playing basketball. He was hanging out on the beach with friends when the local basketball coach asked him to play because he was tall. Since Kukoc knew the coach's sons and the gym was nearby, he joined the practice. Kukoc kept playing and watching tapes of NBA games, especially enjoying the Boston Celtics, the Los Angeles Lakers, and the Detroit Pistons.

He then played on Yugoslavia's national teams from 1989 to 1991. Moving to Italy to play between 1991 and 1993, Kukoc was named European player of the year three times. When he came to the United States in 1993, Kukoc first played for the Chicago Bulls before being traded to other teams, landing in Milwaukee in 2003. He was very excited to come to the NBA and still goes home each summer to spend a day or two sharing his skills at a two-week basketball camp in Split.

Legendary basketball player Drazen Petrovik (1964–1993) grew up and first played ball in Sibenik, a small port city on the Adriatic Sea. As a youngster, he practiced two or three times a day, often shooting more than 500 baskets before he had to go to school in the mornings. He eventually moved on to play professionally, once scoring 112 points in a Croatian League game. He later played in Madrid, Spain, and then came to the United States when he was twenty-five. Petrovik first played for the Portland Trailblazers and then the New Jersey Nets, where he became one of the best shooting guards in the National Basketball Association. With his deadly aim, he averaged more than twenty points per game. Although his career was cut short when he was killed in a car accident in Germany, Drazen was elected to the Basketball Hall of Fame in 2002.

An Afternoon Downtown

ARKO PRELOG LOVED RIDING THE NUMBER 6 TRAM through the streets of his hometown of Zagreb. After school on Fridays he had a job to run errands for his father, who owned a large printing shop near the train station. His mom ran the office, while his dad supervised the technical side of things. The family's company was in the southern part of the sprawling capital city, only a couple of blocks from the fast-moving Sava River. Many of the firm's customers were in Novi Zagreb, on the opposite side of the river, where there were many computer companies. Other customers were in the older parts of the city, both in the exclusive shopping district and near the government buildings.

Sometimes Marko rode his bicycle to make deliveries. One day, he was just as glad to sit on a tram seat and let the driver do the work. Besides, it had started to drizzle and Marko had no wish to get wet.

The dampness didn't seem to bother other people. The streets of Zagreb bustled with shoppers protected by their bright red-and-white striped umbrellas, harried office workers, and laughing kids returning from field trips at one of the city's many museums. The tram rumbled along Praska and crossed Andrije Hebranga, just beyond the Gallery of Modern Art. Marko knew that the American embassy was down the street to the left. As he rode along, he saw the office of Croatia Airlines and could look in the windows of many travel agencies

Opposite: **Zagreb is a busy city with shoppers and business owners alike.**

along this street. Colorful vacation posters were plastered everywhere, advertising trips to Italy, Canada, Germany, and the United States. Marko especially liked looking at pictures of the Dalmatian coast, where he and his parents vacationed every August. He loved camping and swimming. On the opposite side of the avenue were broad parks with benches where strollers could stop to rest. But with the day's light rain, few people paused on their errands.

Trams make their way through Zagreb's city center.

Jelacic Square

Most of the city's trams stopped at Ban Jelacic Square. From Marko's history classes, he knew that the plaza was named after a Croatian hero who defeated the Hungarians in an uprising in 1848. This vast central square of Zagreb's Lower Town was a turnaround and hub for the city's intricate public transportation network. Trams made it easy for Marko to get anywhere he needed to go.

Croatian Holidays

New Year's Day	January 1
Epiphany	January 6
Easter Monday	March or April
Labor Day	May 1
Statehood Day	May 30
Anti-Fascism Day	June 22
Homeland Thanksgiving or Gratitude Day	August 5
Assumption of Mary	August 15
All Saints Day	November 1
Christmas	December 25

Today, Marko's dad wanted him to drop off a box of stationery at Mrs. Boskovic's bookshop on Ilica, the main commercial street. Her shop was near a downtown department store. However, Marko's mom preferred the new Centar Kaptol, a shopping center out of the downtown area that had better parking. Many vacationing Austrians, Germans, and other visitors also shopped there because of the large selection of housewares. Ilica Street ran west from the square and was crowded with rumbling trucks, honking taxis, tiny cars, and trams. In the damp weather, Croatian flags hung limply from tall poles lining the streets. But when the sun was out, the dry flags snapped in the wind, providing a much more colorful display.

Marko always enjoyed visiting Mrs. Boskovic because she told jokes and tipped him for making the deliveries. But the best reason for going there was having another chance to talk with Nina, her daughter. Marko and Nina were thirteen years old. Although they went to different schools, they met one day when their art classes were touring the Gallery of Modern Art. Nina wanted to be a painter and already knew a lot about Mihanovic, Racic, and Bukovac, three notable Croatian artists whose works were among the hundreds displayed at the free gallery. After they met there a few more times while with their school groups, Nina and Marko received permission from their parents to join their friends at the movies on the weekend. They would meet Luka, Milko, Ivan, Josip, and the other guys from Marko's basketball team, as well as some girls from Nina's school.

Sometimes, to act intercontinental, the whole gang munched hamburgers at the McDonald's restaurant on Ilica,

McDonald's is a popular spot for a quick burger.

How to Play "Toothpaste"

Croatian kids play a word game called Kaladont, which means "toothpaste." Five to ten players can join in the fun, which is a good test of their vocabulary. The first player begins the game with one word, such as *mouse*. The second player then needs to find a word beginning with the last two letters of mouse. *Sentence* might be a good choice, using the *se* to start. Of course, those are English words, and Croatian would naturally be used in Zagreb or Split. Everybody in the group has a turn, and anyone not finding a correct word is out of the game. The game keeps going until there is one winner. But nobody is supposed to end a word with the letters *ka*. If that happens, the next player will immediately say "kaladont," which also ends the game. Such word games remain popular even in the eye of television.

although they all preferred *cevapcici*, Croatia's traditional spicy pork or beef meatballs served at small local restaurants. Or they simply grabbed a snack in the cafeteria of the sports club where the boys played basketball. All the kids looked forward to getting older so that they could hang out in a coffeehouse like the Bulldog Café on Bogoviceva Street, where the university and art crowd gathered. Until then, they settled for hot chocolate and talked about their teachers, sports, homework, and parents while watching the passing crowds. Everyone loved walking in Zagreb because it was so easy to get around the tree-lined streets.

Seeing the Twin Spires

Marko moved quickly when he swung down from the tram and edged into the crowded flow of pedestrians. The box he carried was not that heavy, only some letterheads and envelopes. Marko easily made his way along the street to Mrs. Boskovic's. To the north, he saw the twin spires of the old

Market shoppers check the fresh produce under the twin spires of the old cathedral.

cathedral. The Archbishop's Palace was attached to the imposing cathedral's ornate stonework. But Marko had never met the archbishop. He and his family attended mass at Saint Mark's in Gornji Grad, the Upper City. On the east side of the square where the archbishop's church was located was the Sabor, the Croatian parliament building. From one of its windows in 1919, a proclamation had been read, announcing that Croatia was splitting away from Austro-Hungarian Empire. On the opposite side of the church was the Presidential Palace, where Croatian viceroys once lived. Marko was always impressed with all the history when he came to the neighborhood.

Off to Karlovac

Nina wasn't at the shop when Marko arrived. He had forgotten that she had gone to the city of Karlovac, south of Zagreb, to visit her cousin for the weekend. Disappointed, Marko dropped off the stationery, listened to a few jokes just to be polite, and then left the store. He was hoping to tell his girlfriend about the new rock CD by Zagreb's Nenad Bach that his pal Ivan had loaned him at school.

Marko purchased another tram ticket, a *tramvajska karta*, for the ride home. At the newspaper kiosk where he bought his ticket, Marko looked over the colorful display of magazines and newspapers. Bold headlines jumped from the racks, calling attention to their stories. Before making a selection to read on the ride back to the print shop, Marko thumbed through a copy of *Hollywood*. He scanned an interview with *Lord of the Rings* movie star Elijah Wood and checked the latest on the action blockbuster *Terminator 3*.

Marko passed up *Golf Digest Croatia* to check out the body builders peering from the cover of *Fitness* magazine. He then bought a copy of *Magazin Koskara*. He found a great story on basketball star Nikola Vujcic, a power forward with Maccabi Tel Aviv in Israel. Marko loved basketball. He and his dad often went to the Drazen Petrovik Basketball Centre to cheer for their home team, Cibona.

Since he was tall and lanky with quick moves, Marko played center and hoped someday to be as good a three-point shooter as Vujcic. City teams, not those of schools, are the primary source of basketball development in Croatia. Each year,

What to Wear?

For day-to-day activities, Croatian young people dress just like kids in the West. Blue jeans and sweatshirts are popular for casual wear all year. Boys put on sport coats when going to church or other special occasions, and girls wear dresses. In the winter, heavy coats, gloves, and hats keep out the cold mountain wind.

Traditional clothing is still sometimes worn for festivals or pageants. Almost every town and village has its individual styles. Costumes in northern Croatia are richer and more finely made than in some of the poorer areas of the country. Along the warm Adriatic coastline, the costumes are made with lighter textiles.

The area around Zagreb is called Šestine. Therefore, costumes from this region are also called "Šestinska nošnja." Red, white, and black are the pre-

dominant colors. Boys wear white shirts and either red or black vests. Their white trousers are held up by brown leather belts hand tooled with intricate designs. They also wear black boots and black hats that are similar to a derby. In other parts of Croatia, boys wear brown and black slippers instead of boots. The girls wear red head scarfs and aprons in addition to their full dresses and white blouses.

According to legend, the necktie originated in Croatia. One story is that the French emperor Napoleon favored the scarves worn by Croatian soldiers who fought with his army when he invaded Russia in 1812. Yet the French link goes back even further into history when thousands of Croatian mercenaries hired out to King Louis XIV, who ruled France between 1643 and 1715. These skilled fighters wore scarves whose design was copied by officers in the French court. The Croatian word for neckcloth, *kravata*, slowly evolved into the French *cravate* and eventually became the English cravat.

Boys play a friendly game of basketball.

400 to 500 kids try out for a place on the Zagreb city team. Marko was already good enough to be among the final hundred selected. From these kids, a city team would be formed, so Marko was working very hard to be one of them.

Actually, Marko would rather have been practicing his jump shots instead of delivering packages. But the money from his after-school job enabled him to buy sports magazines. Vujcic, one of Marko's heroes, led the under-sixteen and under-eighteen Croatian national teams to first-place victories in European basketball championships in the mid-1990s. Vujcic went on to play internationally.

Ready for Pizza

Marko climbed into the tram for his ride home, just as it was starting to sprinkle again. The ticket machine validated his karta with a ka-ching, and the tram started for a rollicking ride back to his parents' shop. Looking out at the rain through the steamed-over tram window, Marko began daydreaming: "Someday, I'm going to play pro ball and maybe even go to America." But he shook himself awake. He was eager to see his dad and mom, because after work they had promised to take him to supper at Pizzicato in the Academy of Music. It was the best pizza place in town. And tomorrow was Saturday, with plenty of time for basketball practice. What more could he want?

I'm Hungry!

Breakfast for Croatian kids seems to North Americans more like lunch. They usually eat hearty open-faced sandwiches made of homemade white bread, along with smoked bacon or paté, a meat spread. If they are really hungry, slabs of cheese and tomato slices are added. Sometimes cream cheese is spread on the bread. Lunch is much the same, but supper is more elaborate, usually featuring lots of vegetables. Cuisine varies throughout the country, with fish and seafood popular on the coast. Regional items such as heavy, paprika-seasoned sausages are eaten in eastern Slavonia. In north-central Croatia, grilled lamb (*janje*) or pork (*svinjetina*) is often served for dinner. Many of the islands have their specialties, such as a very hard cheese from Pag. Spaghetti and other pasta dishes are popular and filling, reflecting an Italian influence. For a Hungarian touch, everyone enjoys goulash (*gulas*) and thin pancakes rolled up around a filling of sweet berry jam and topped with creamy dark chocolate (*palacinka*). *Burek*, a thick pastry stuffed with meat or cheese, can be eaten on the run like some American fast foods. Croatian food reflects the influences of the different cultures that once held sway here, from the Italians to the French and everyone else in between. Croatians are proud of their cuisine, which emphasizes fresh, healthy ingredients.

Timeline

Croatian History		World History	
		2500 B.C.	Egyptians build the Pyramids and the Sphinx in Giza.
The first Greek colonies are founded along the Adriatic coast.	c. 580 B.C.	563 B.C.	The Buddha is born in India.
Romans rule the east coast of the Adriatic.	After 300 B.C.		
Roman emperor Diocletian lives in present-day Split.	A.D. 305	A.D. 313	The Roman emperor Constantine recognizes Christianity.
Croats start moving to what is today's Croatia.	Early 600s	610	The Prophet Muhammad begins preaching a new religion called Islam.
Duke Trpimir issues a charter mentioning the name Croatia, the first time it is used in official documents.	852		
Tomislav becomes the first Croatian king, ruling over Pannonia and Dalmatian Croatia.	925		
		1054	The Eastern (Orthodox) and Western (Roman) Churches break apart.
		1066	William the Conqueror defeats the English in the Battle of Hastings.
Croatia joins a union with Hungary; Prince Koloman is crowned king of Croatia, Slavonia, and Dalmatia.	1102	1095	Pope Urban II proclaims the First Crusade.
Croatian nobles force King Andrija II (Andrew II) to issue a document called the Golden Bull that limits the royal authority.	1222	1215	King John seals the Magna Carta.
Croatia has civil wars.	1300s	1300s	The Renaissance begins in Italy.
		1347	The Black Death sweeps through Europe.
Turks invade Croatia.	1433	1453	Ottoman Turks capture Constantinople, conquering the Byzantine Empire.
		1492	Columbus arrives in North America.
The Habsburg dynasty takes over the Croatian throne.	1527	1500s	The Reformation leads to the birth of Protestantism.
Croatia is liberated from the Turks; inland Croatia remains under the rule of the Habsburgs while Venice controls the Adriatic coast and islands except for the Dubrovnik Republic.	1699	1776	The Declaration of Independence is signed.

Croatian History

After the short rule of the French under Napoleon, who defeated Venice and dissolved the Dubrovnik Republic, almost all of current Croatian territory becomes part of the Habsburg monarchy.	1815
Croatian becomes the official language of Croatia.	1847
Josip Jelacic defeats the Hungarians and reunites Croatia.	1848
World War I ends; Croatia becomes part of the Kingdom of Serbs, Croats, and Slovenes, later to be named Yugoslavia.	1918
Popular Croatian politician Stjepan Radić is assassinated.	1928
Yugoslav King Alexander unites Croatia with its neighbors, separating the Serbs and the Slovenes.	1929
German and Italian forces occupy Yugoslavia; resistance is led by Josip Broz Tito.	1941
The Federative Socialist Republic of Yugoslavia is proclaimed; Croatia becomes one of its federal republics.	1945
Tito, the head of Yugoslavia, dies.	1980
The first multiparty elections after World War II are held; the Croatian Assembly elects strongman Franjo Tudjman as its first president.	1990
Croatia proclaims independence; the Serbian rebellion starts, supported by the Yugoslav Army; a third of Croatia is occupied.	1991
Peace accords are signed, ending the Bosnian conflict.	1995

World History

1789	The French Revolution begins.
1865	The American Civil War ends.
1914	World War I breaks out.
1917	The Bolshevik Revolution brings communism to Russia.
1929	Worldwide economic depression begins.
1939	World War II begins, following the German invasion of Poland.
1945	World War II ends.
1957	The Vietnam War starts.
1969	Humans land on the moon.
1975	The Vietnam War ends.
1979	Soviet Union invades Afghanistan.
1983	Drought and famine in Africa.
1989	The Berlin Wall is torn down, as communism crumbles in Eastern Europe.
1991	Soviet Union breaks into separate states.
1992	Bill Clinton is elected U.S. president.
2000	George W. Bush is elected U.S. president.
2001	Terrorists attack World Trade Towers, New York, and the Pentagon, Washington, D.C.

Fast Facts

Official name: Republic of Croatia (Republika Hrvatska)

Capital: Zagreb

Official language: Croatian

Trogir

Croatia's flag

Plant life

Year of founding:	1991
Major religion:	Roman Catholic
National anthem:	"Our Beautiful Homeland" ("Lijepa nasa domovino")
Government:	Parliamentary democracy
Chief of state:	President
Head of government:	Prime minister
Area:	21,825 square miles (56,542 sq km)
Latitude and longitude:	45° 10' N, 15° 30' E
Borders:	Slovenia, Hungary, Serbia and Montenegro, and Bosnia and Herzegovina
Highest elevation:	Dinaric Mountains, 6,004 feet (1,830 m)
Lowest elevation:	Sea level
Average winter temperature:	30F° to 86°F (-1°C to 30°C) in the continental region, 23°F to 32°F (-5°C to 0°C) in the mountain region, and 41°F to 50°F (5°C to 10°C) in the coastal region.
Average summer temperature:	72°F to 79°F (22°C to 26°C) in the continental region, 59°F to 68°F (15°C to 20°C) in the mountain region, and 79°F to 86°F (26°C to 30°C) in the coastal region.
National population:	4,428,000 (2003 est.)

Plitvice lakes

Croatian currency

Population of major cities (2004 est):

Zagreb	1,081,000
Split	172,700
Rijeka	141,800
Osijelk	89,200
Zadar	68,600
Dubrovnik	30,000

Famous landmarks:
- ▶ *Emperor Diocletian's palace*, Split
- ▶ *Krk Island*
- ▶ *Plitvice Lakes National Park*
- ▶ *Adriatric Sea coastline*
- ▶ *Velebit Alps*

Industry: Croatia has an extensive manufacturing sector, with chemicals and plastics among its most important products. Its factories also turn out tools, fabricated metal, electronic devices, pig iron, and rolled steel products. Shipbuilding is another major industry, as are petroleum refining and the manufacture of food products and beverages. Tourists are attracted to the country's historical and natural features and love the sunny Adriatic coastline. Its major trading partners are Italy, Germany, and Bosnia and Herzegovina.

Currency: Kuna, divided into 100 lipa.
In May 2004, U.S.$1 = 6.07 kuna

System of weights and measures: The metric system is Croatia's official system.

Literacy rate: 98.5 percent

School children

Common Words and Phrases:

Zdravo	hello
Dovidenja	good-bye
Da	yes
Ne	no
Molim	please
Hvala	thank you
Govorite li engleski?	Do you speak English?
Kako ti je ime?	What's your name?
Moje ime je _____.	My name is _____.
Odakle ste?	Where are you from?
Ja sam iz Kanade.	I am from Canada.
Ja sam iz Amerike.	I am from the United States.

Famous Croats:

Ivan Mestrovic		(1883–1962)
Sculptor		
Drazen Petrovik		(1964–1993)
Professional basketball player		
Vladimir Prelog		(1906–1998)
Chemist		
Stjepan Radić		(1871–1928)
Nationalist leader		
Cardinal Alojzije Stepinac		(1898–1960)
Church leader		
Bishop Josip Juraj Strossmajer		(1815–1905)
Founder of the Academy of Sciences and Arts and Zagreb University		

Cardinal Alojzije Stepinac

To Find Out More

Nonfiction

▶ Cooper, Robert. *Croatia* (Cultures of the World). Tarrytown, NY: Benchmark Books, 2000.

▶ Ellis, Roger. *New International Plays for Young Audiences: Plays of Cultural Conflict*. Colorado Springs, CO: Meriwether Publishing Ltd., 2002.

▶ Gabrielpillai, Matilda. *Bosnia/Herzegovina* (Countries of the World). Milwaukee, WI: Gareth Stevens, 2002.

▶ Marcovitz, Hal. *The Balkans: People in Conflict*. Broomall, PA: Chelsea House Library, 2002.

▶ Milivojevic, JoAnn. *Bosnia and Herzegovina* (Enchantment of the World). Danbury, CT: Children's Press, 2004.

▶ Milivojevic, JoAnn. *Serbia, Rev. Ed.* (Enchantment of the World). Danbury, CT: Children's Press, 2003.

▶ Pavlovic, Zoran, and Gritzner, Charles F. *Modern World Nations: Croatia*. Broomall, PA: Chelsea House Library, 2002.

Web Sites

▶ **Croatian National Tourist Board**
http://www.croatia.hr
Contains information on the geography, tourist attractions, history, and culture of Croatia.

▶ **Hrvartski**
http://www.hr/darko/etf/et22.html
Learn about famous Croatian scientists and other notable personalities throughout the country's history.

▶ **President of Croatia**
http://www.predsjednik.hr/
*Read a biography of the Croatian
president and explore links to various
branches of the Croatian government.*

▶ **Croatian Music Society—
Tamburica**
http://www.geocities.com/
tamburica_vorarlberg/english/
costumes.htm
*Admire traditional Croatian clothing,
with photos showing samples from
different areas of the country.*

▶ **Croatian Football Federation**
http://www.hns-cff.hr
*Find the latest details on soccer
in Croatia.*

▶ **CIA World Fact Book**
http://www.cia.gov/cia/publications/
factbook/geos/hr.html
*Up-to-date geographic, economic,
government, and social information
about Croatia.*

Organizations and Embassies

▶ **Embassy of Croatia**
2343 Massachusetts Avenue, NW
Washington, D.C. 20008
202-588-5899

▶ **Ministry of Tourism**
Ulica grada Vukovara 78
10 000 Zagreb, Croatia
182-142

Index

Page numbers in *italics* indicate illustrations.

Meet the Author

Martin Hintz has written numerous books for Children's Press. For this book he traveled around Croatia, visiting Zagreb, Dubrovnik, Split, and other cities in this marvelous country. He toured museums, hiked trails, dangled his toes in the Adriatic, ate great amounts of delicious food, and drove through dramatic mountain passes. Hintz talked with truck drivers, historians, tour guides, politicians, and many young Croats who helped shape his understanding of the country and its people.

His research also included visiting his local library to find books on Croatian history and culture. He read traveler's guidebooks and looked over books of photographs that showcased the countryside and its cities. In addition, Hintz reviewed videotapes that were helpful in describing places he had not been able to visit. Hintz also found that surfing the Internet was very helpful in finding little-known facts about the country.

Hintz is a past president and board chairman of the Society of American Travel Writers, and belongs to the Society of Professional Journalists and other journalism associations. He lives near Milwaukee, Wisconsin, with his wife Pam. They raise chickens on their small farm and have a pet hen named Doris that has been featured in books and television.

Photo Credits

Photographs © 2004:

AKG-Images, London: 47;
AP/Wide World Photos: 57, 73 (Darko Bandic), 60 (Antonio Bat), 115 (J. Pat Carter), 114 (Michel Euler), 53, 113 (Michel Lipchitz), 112 (Michael Probst), 93 (Damjan Tadic), 56;
Art Resource, NY: 41 (Cameraphoto), 44 (Giraudon), 43 (Scala);
Brown Brothers: 48, 49, 133 bottom;
Bruce Coleman Inc.: 26 (J.C. Carton), 125 left, 125 right (Lee Foster);
Corbis Images: 87 (Alinari Archives), 42 (Archivo Iconografico, S.A.), 89, 104 (Bettmann), 16, 20, 30 bottom, 33, 69, 78, 82, 83, 97, 106, 133 top (Jonathan Blair), 36, 126 (Ed Kashi), 74, 99, 130 (Richard Klune), 123 (Otto Lang), 54 (Jacques Langevin), 32 right (Joe McDonald), 52 (Emmanuel Ortiz), 65 (Tim Page), 22, 111 bottom (Reuters), 64 (Joel W. Rogers), 29 (Jeffrey L. Rotman), 17 (Janez Skok), 8 (Milena Soree), 71 (Tim Thompson), 58 bottom (Peter Turnley), 46 (Underwood & Underwood), 11, 75 (Nik Wheeler);
Corbis SABA/Bernard Bisson: 50 right;
Corbis Sygma/Julio Donoso: 107;
Getty Images/AFP: 50 left, 95;
Hulton I Archive/Getty Images: 12;
Panos Pictures: 70 (IPA), 24 (Matjaz Kacicnik), 91, 92 (Matjaz Kacicnik/ IPA), 9 (G. Wrona);

Peter Arnold Inc.: 15 (Fred Bruemmer), 38 (Thomas Ernsting/Bilderberg);
Photo Researchers, NY: 32 left (Manfred Danegger/OKAPIA), 34 (Hermann Eisenbeiss);
Photri Inc./RRP: 86;
PictureQuest/Wegner/Premium Stock: 31;
Sovfoto/Eastfoto/RIA-NOVOSTI: 51;
Superstock, Inc.: 101 (Croatian Museum of Native Art, *"Rest at Noon Time"*, by Ivan Generalic), 28 top (James Urbach), 63, 90, 119 (Steve Vidler), 28 bottom, 39, 80;
The Image Works: 7 bottom, 76 (Hideo Haga/HAGA), 25 (Marcel Eva Malherbe), 30 top (Josef Polleross);
Tim Thompson: 127;
Transit Photo and Archive: 37, 72, 84, 131 (Peter Hirth), 19 top (Christian Nowak), cover, 2, 111 top (Silke Rötting);
TRIP Photo Library: 7 top, 14, 35 (A Alborno), 58 top, 67, 68, 105, 118, 121, 132 bottom (M Barlow), 116 (Martin Barlow/Art Directors), 100, 109 (T Bognar), 45 (Tibor Bognar/Art Directors), 19 bottom, 132 top (F Torrance), 96 (Nick & Janet Wiseman/Art Directors).

Maps by XNR Productions Inc.